dorkboy™ comics presents...

Kernel Corn & Peater™ the black eyed pea©

ROTTEN VEGETABLES

by damian willcox

published by dorkboy comics
www.dorkboycomics.com

I0153553

contact: damian@dorkboycomics.com

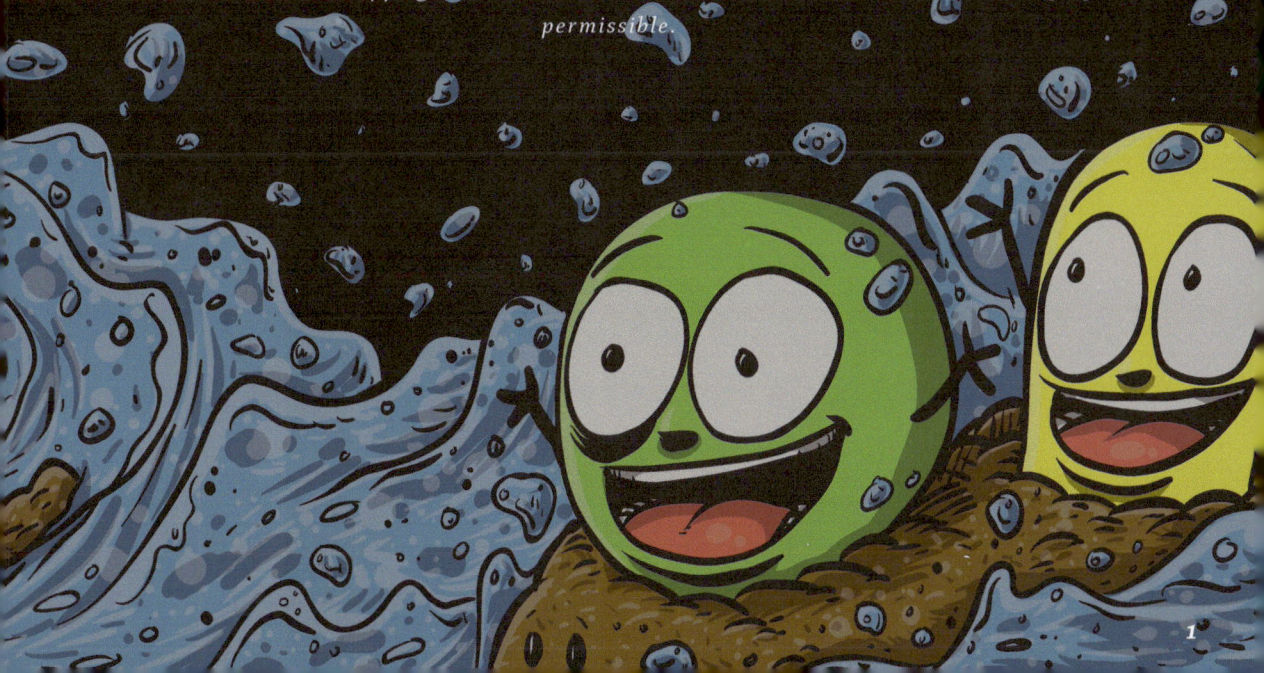

Introduction

I would like to say that Kernel Corn and Peater the Black Eyed Pea were thrust into this world when the cataclysmic passing of a meteor met with an aimlessly wandering shuttle craft containing canned vegetables, but that is sadly incorrect. In fact, were it that simple many questions and expectations of these two vegetables would be laid to rest indefinitely.

Truthfully however, these two unassuming cohorts came wandering into existence quite organically ...and accidentally.

It started out with a few random black and white "corny" (pardon the pun, but then again if i need to say that now, you should probably close this book) comics whose drawings were equally as bad as the puns they communicated. A few comics later they really started developing their own distinct personalities (vegetabalities?), but it wasn't until I coloured their world that they really came into being. This is where the larger "Life of Fibre" story you hold in your hands began....

What was originally intended as a "funny" one time comic with a dual purpose (One - bettering the world by explaining how fibre works in the human body with our vegetable heroes as the educators, and Two - pacifying and hopefully ending a good friend's constant requests that I draw a comic about poop and/ or animate a flushing toilet on my website) quickly took on a life of its own.

Quite honestly this story wrote itself, and beneath the thin veneers of the shunned and taboo topic of the digestive system and bad puns is a fun and heartfelt tale of friendship, loyalty and growth.

I can't tell you how much I enjoyed making the comics you are about to read, and I just hope you enjoy reading this book as much as I did putting it together.

♥damian

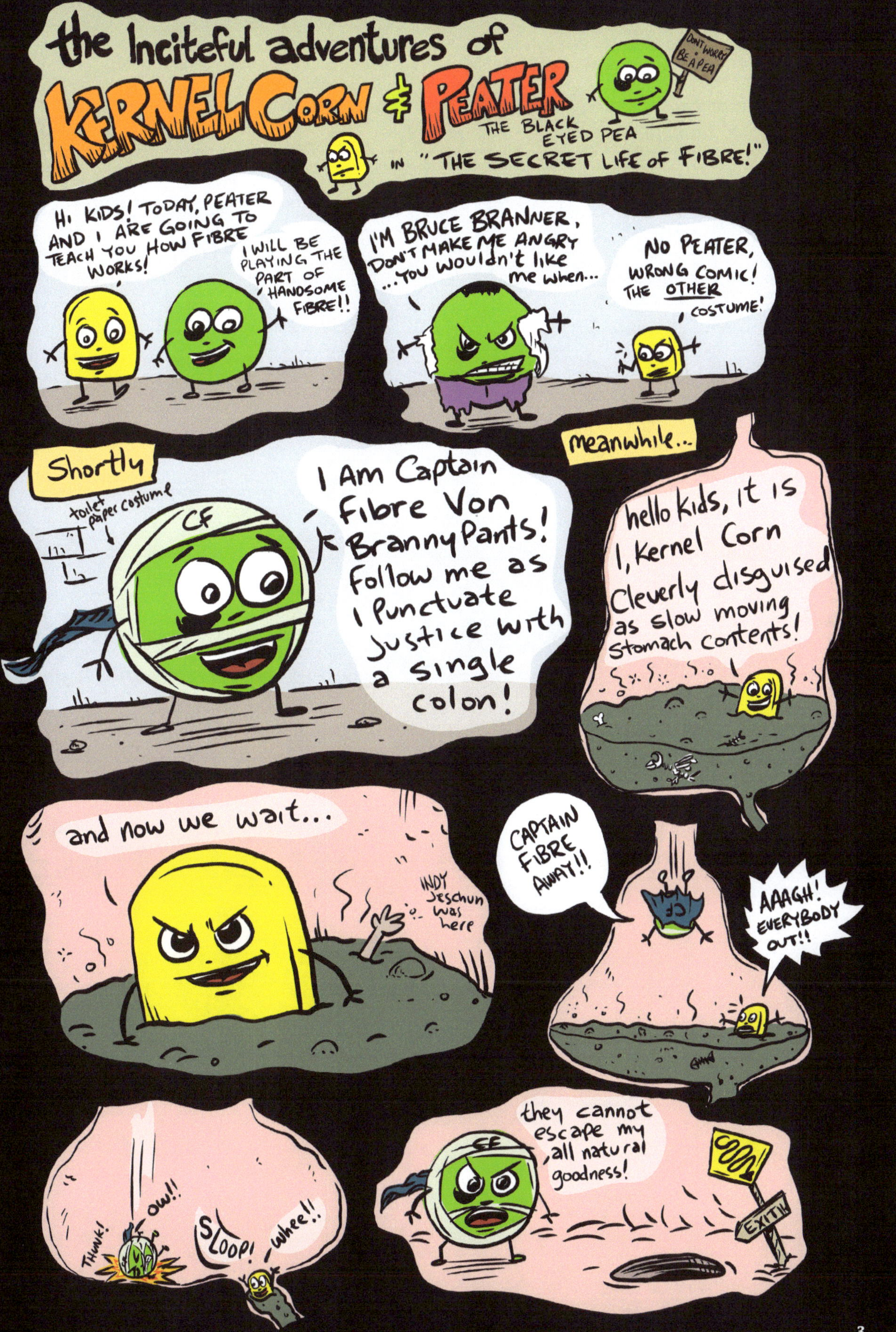

the Inciteful adventures of
KERNEL CORN & PEATER THE BLACK EYED PEA
DON'T WORRY BE A PEA
IN "THE SECRET LIFE of FIBRE!"
HI KIDS! TODAY, PEATER AND I ARE GOING TO TEACH YOU HOW FIBRE WORKS!
I WILL BE PLAYING THE PART OF HANDSOME FIBRE!!
I'M BRUCE BRANNER, DON'T MAKE ME ANGRY ...YOU wouldn't like me when...
NO PEATER, WRONG COMIC! THE OTHER COSTUME!
Shortly
toilet paper costume
CF
I Am Captain Fibre Von Branny Pants! Follow me as I Punctuate Justice with a single colon!
meanwhile...
hello kids, it is I, Kernel Corn Cleverly disguised as slow moving stomach contents!
and now we wait...
INDY Jeschun was here
CAPTAIN FIBRE AWAY!!
CF
AAAGH! EVERYBODY OUT!!
THWK!
OW!!
SLOOP!
whee!!
they cannot escape my all natural goodness!
CF
EXIT

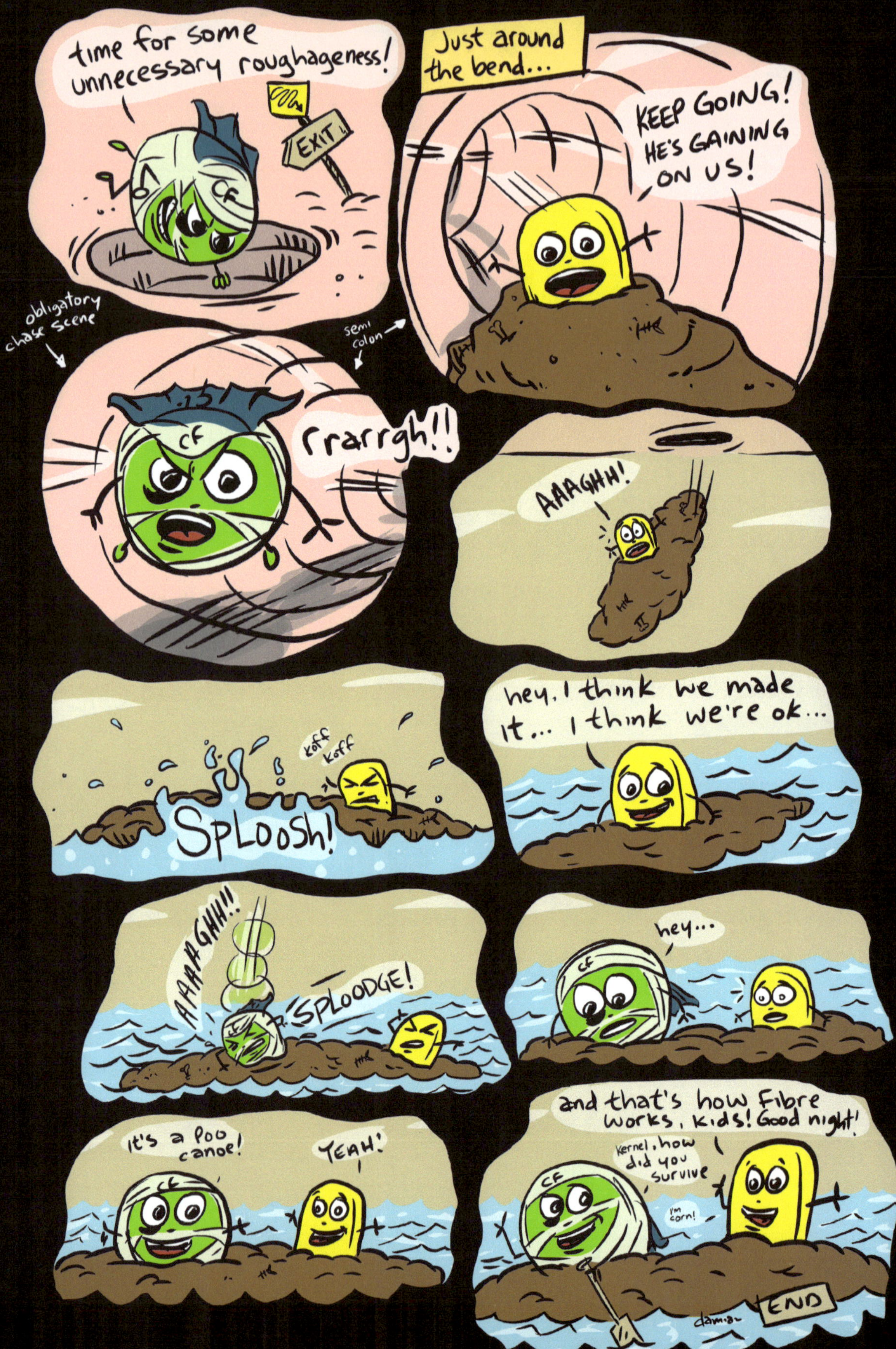
time for some unnecessary roughageness!
EXIT
Just around the bend...
KEEP GOING! HE'S GAINING ON US!
obligatory chase scene
semi colon
rrarrgh!!
AAAGHH!
koff koff
SPLOOSH!
hey, I think we made it... I think we're ok...
AAAAGHH!!
SPLOODGE!
hey...
it's a poo canoe!
YEAH!
and that's how fibre works, kids! Good night!
kernel, how did you survive
I'm corn!
END

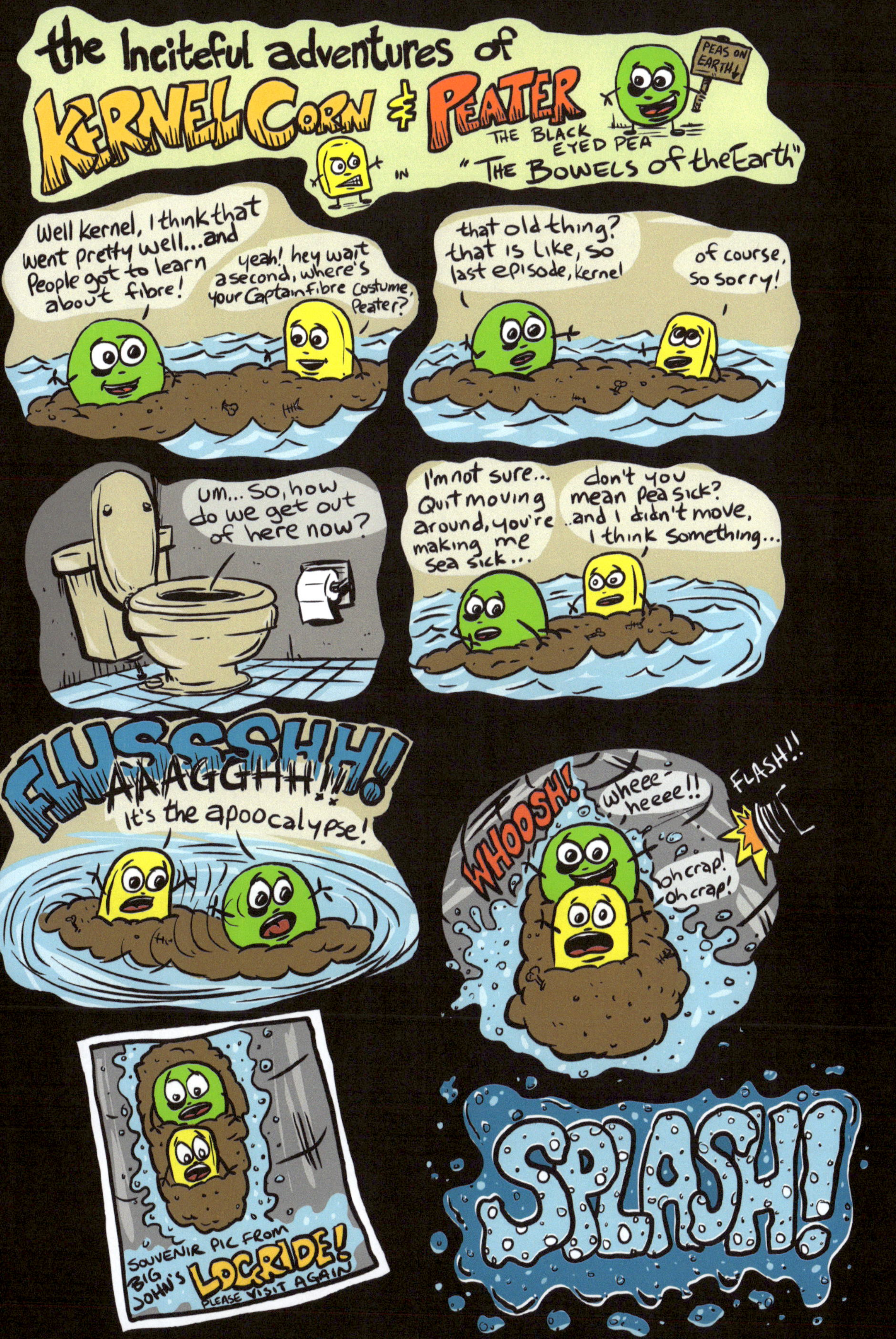
the Inciteful adventures of
KERNEL CORN & PEATER THE BLACK EYED PEA
IN "THE BOWELS of the Earth"
PEAS ON EARTH
Well kernel, I think that went pretty well...and People got to learn about fibre!
yeah! hey wait a second, where's your Captain fibre costume, Peater?
that old thing? that is like, so last episode, kernel
of course, so sorry!
um... so, how do we get out of here now?
I'm not sure... Quit moving around, you're making me sea sick...
don't you mean pea sick? ..and I didn't move, I think something...
FLUSSSHH!
AAAGGHH!!
it's the apoocalypse!
WHOOSH!
wheee-heeee!!
FLASH!!
oh crap! oh crap!
SOUVENIR PIC FROM BIG JOHN'S LOGRIDE! PLEASE VISIT AGAIN
SPLASH!

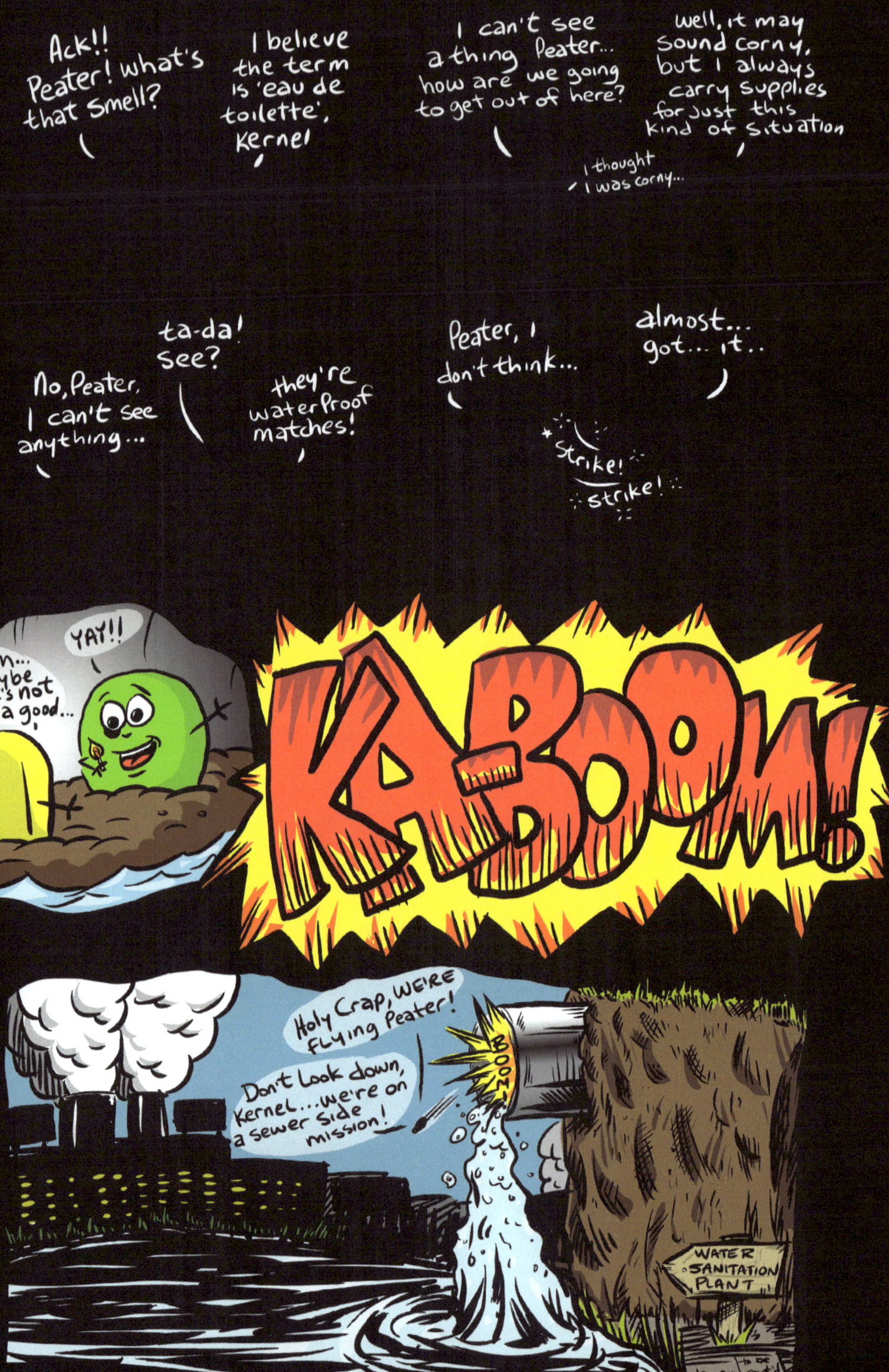

Ack!! Peater! what's that Smell?
I believe the term is 'eau de toilette', Kernel
I can't see a thing Peater... how are we going to get out of here?
well, it may sound corny, but I always carry supplies for just this kind of situation
I thought I was corny...
No, Peater, I can't see anything...
ta-da! see?
they're waterproof matches!
Peater, I don't think...
almost... got... it..
strike!
strike!
um... maybe that's not such a good...
YAY!!
KA-BOOM!
Holy Crap, WE'RE FLYING Peater!
Don't Look down, Kernel... we're on a sewer side mission!
BOOM!
WATER SANITATION PLANT

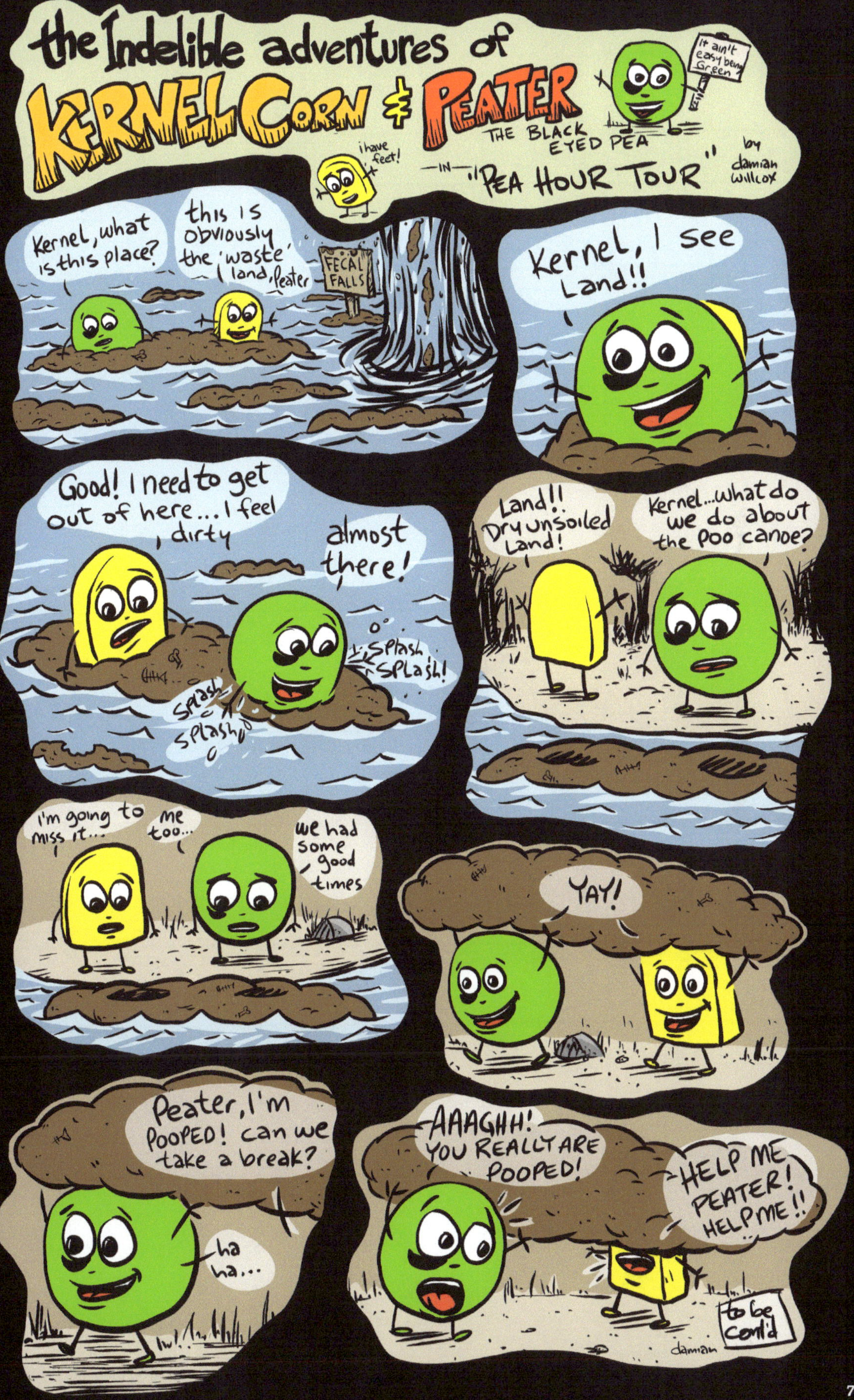
the Indelible adventures of
KERNEL CORN & PEATER THE BLACK EYED PEA
It ain't easy being Green
i have feet!
-IN- "PEA HOUR TOUR"
by damian willcox
Kernel, what is this place?
this is obviously the 'waste' land, Peater
FECAL FALLS
Kernel, I see Land!!
Good! I need to get out of here... I feel dirty
almost there!
Splash Splash!
Splash Splash
Land!! Dry unsoiled Land!
Kernel...what do we do about the Poo canoe?
I'm going to miss it...
me too...
we had some good times
YAY!
Peater, I'm POOPED! can we take a break?
ha ha...
AAAGHH! YOU REALLY ARE POOPED!
HELP ME PEATER! HELP ME!!
to be cont'd
damian

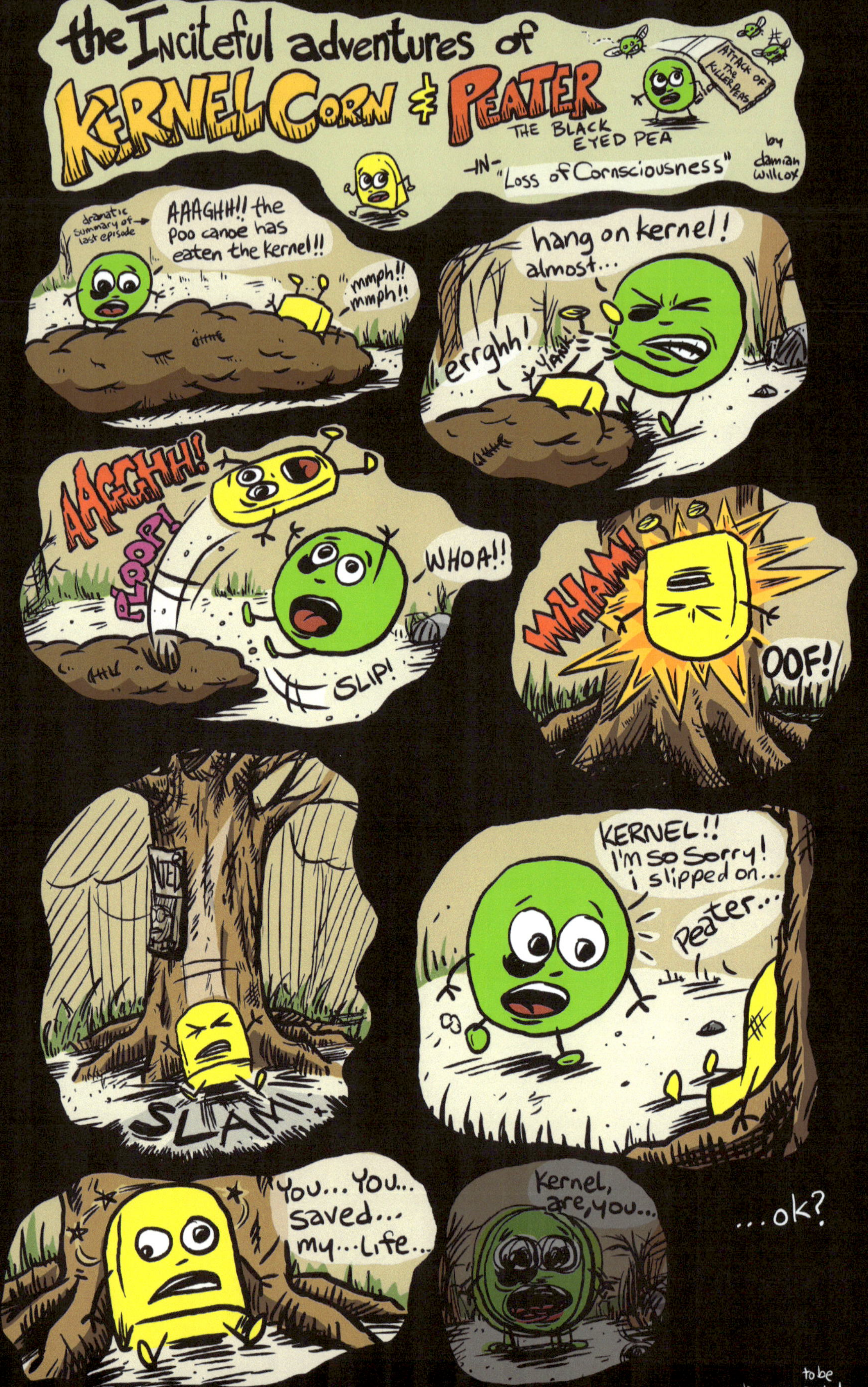

the Inciteful adventures of
KERNEL CORN & PEATER
THE BLACK EYED PEA
-IN- "Loss of Cornsciousness"
by damian willcox
ATTACK OF THE KILLER PEAS
dramatic summary of last episode
AAAGHH!! the poo canoe has eaten the kernel!!
mmph!! mmph!!
hang on kernel! almost...
errghh!
YANK!
AAGGHH!
PLOOP!
WHOA!!
SLIP!
WHAM!
OOF!
SLAM
KERNEL!! I'm so Sorry! i slipped on...
Peater...
You... You... saved... my... Life...
Kernel, are, you...
...ok?
damian
to be cont'd...

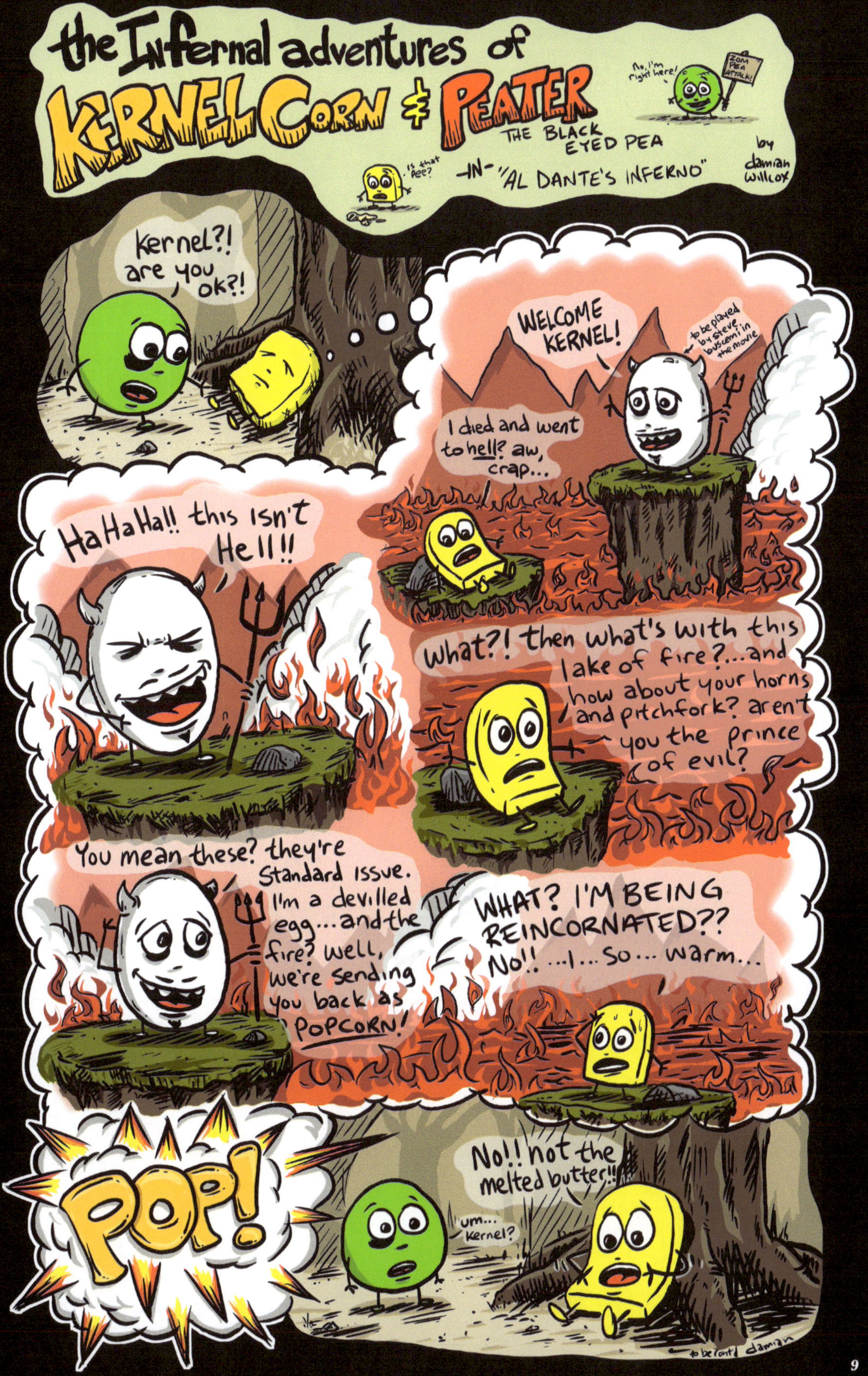
the Infernal adventures of
KERNEL CORN & PEATER
THE BLACK EYED PEA
No, I'm right here!
ZOM PEA ATTACK!
is that pee?
-IN- "AL DANTE'S INFERNO"
by damian willcox
kernel?! are you ok?!
WELCOME KERNEL!
to be played by steve buscemi in the movie
I died and went to hell? aw, crap...
HaHaHa!! this isn't Hell!!
What?! then what's with this lake of fire?...and how about your horns and pitchfork? aren't you the prince of evil?
You mean these? they're standard issue. I'm a devilled egg...and the fire? well, we're sending you back as POPCORN!
WHAT? I'M BEING REINCORNATED?? No!! ...I... so... warm...
POP!
No!! not the melted butter!!
um... kernel?
to be cont'd damian

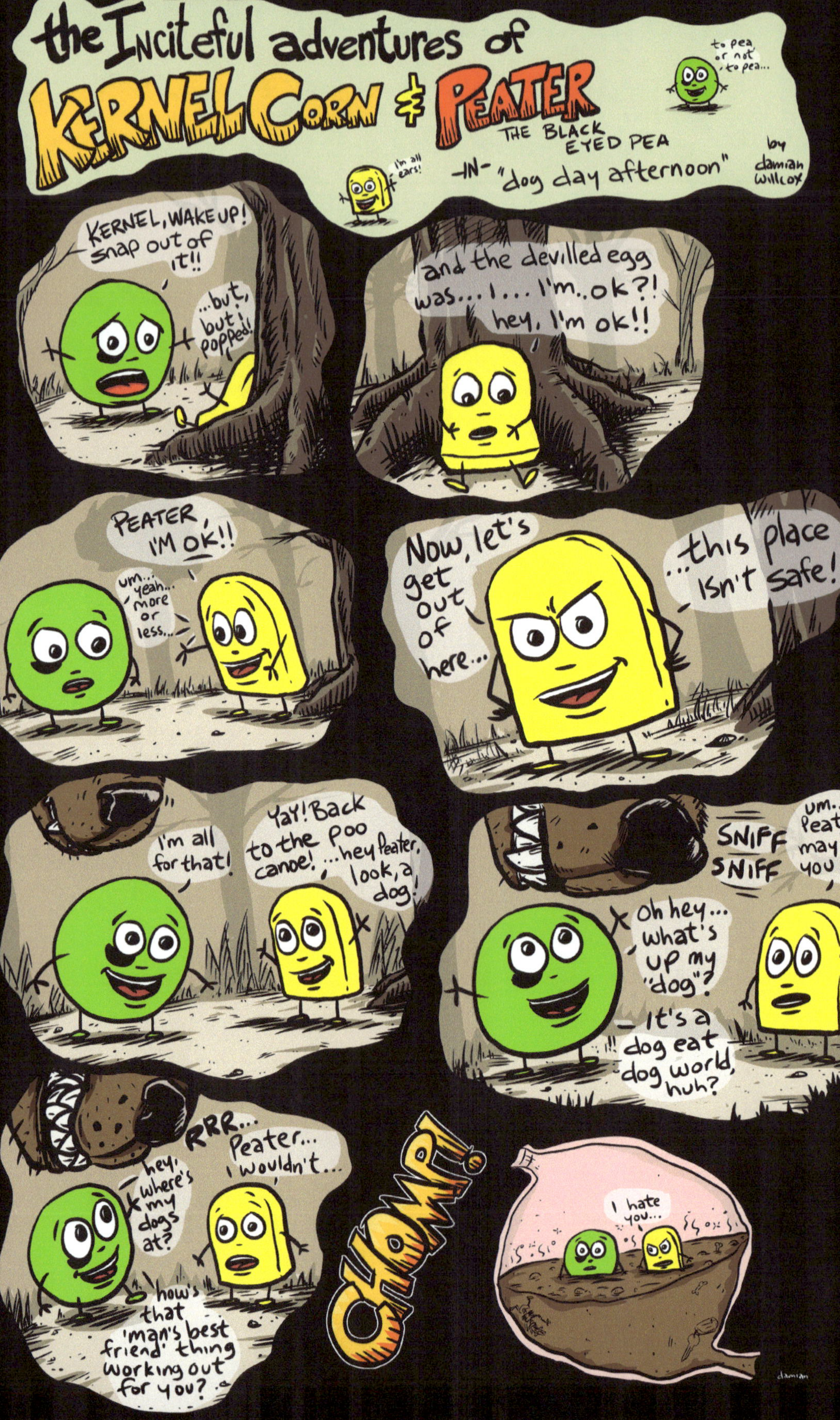
the Inciteful adventures of
KERNEL CORN & PEATER THE BLACK EYED PEA
to pea or not to pea...
I'm all ears!
-IN- "dog day afternoon"
by damian willcox
KERNEL, WAKE UP! snap out of it!!
...but, but I popped!
and the devilled egg was... I... I'm..ok?! hey, I'm ok!!
PEATER, I'M OK!!
um... yeah... more or less...
Now, let's get out of here...
...this place isn't safe!
I'm all for that!
YAY! Back to the poo canoe! ...hey Peater, look, a dog!
SNIFF SNIFF
um... Peater, maybe you should...
Oh hey... what's up my "dog"?
It's a dog eat dog world, huh?
RRR...
hey, where's my dogs at?
Peater... wouldn't...
how's that 'man's best friend' thing working out for you?
CHOMP!!
I hate you...
damian

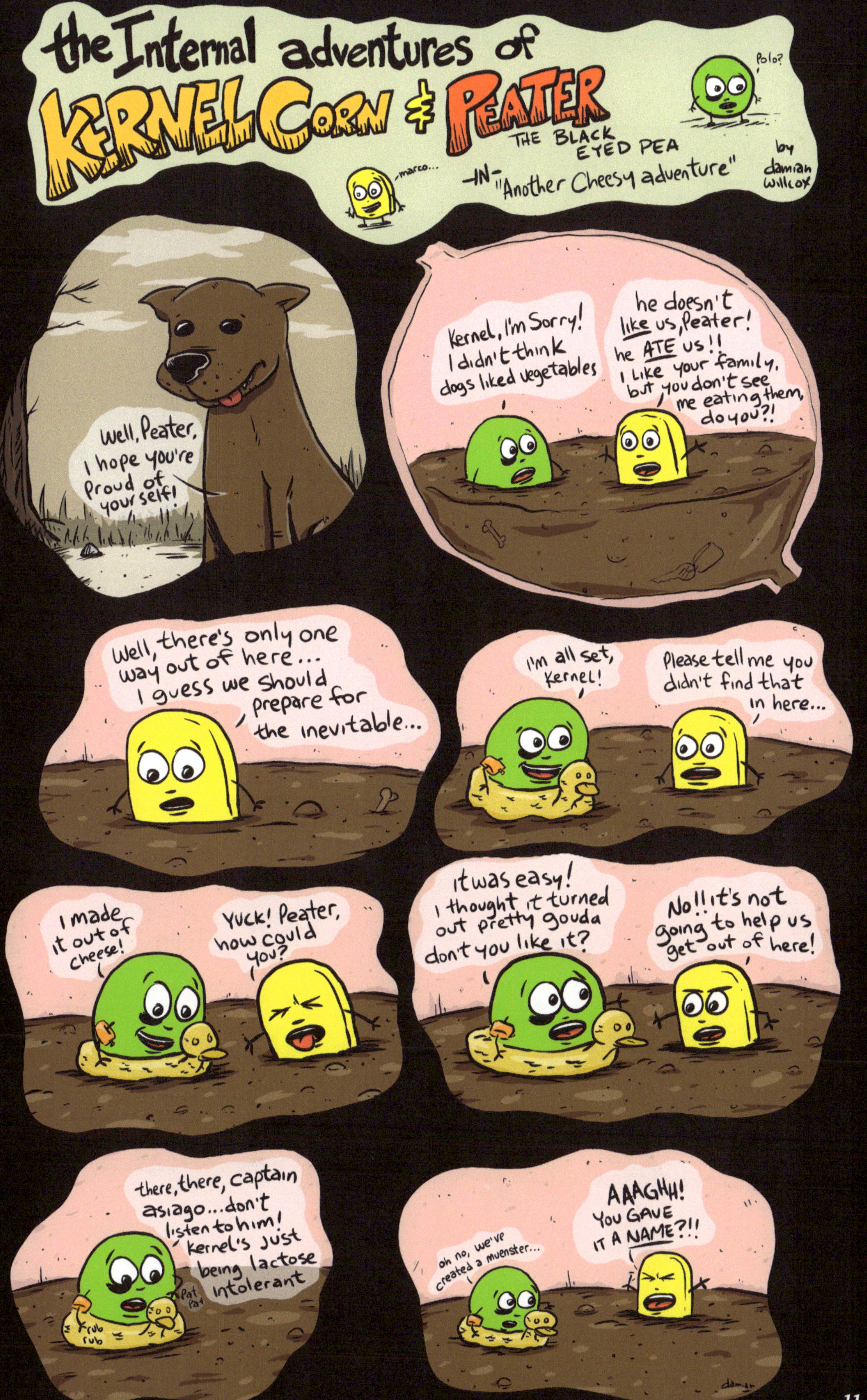

the Internal adventures of
KERNEL CORN & PEATER
THE BLACK EYED PEA
Polo?
marco...
-IN- "Another Cheesy adventure"
by damian willcox
Well, Peater, I hope you're proud of yourself!
Kernel, I'm Sorry! I didn't think dogs liked vegetables
he doesn't like us, Peater! he ATE us!! I like your family, but you don't see me eating them, do you?!
Well, there's only one way out of here... I guess we should prepare for the inevitable...
I'm all set, Kernel!
Please tell me you didn't find that in here...
I made it out of cheese!
Yuck! Peater, how could you?
it was easy! I thought it turned out pretty gouda don't you like it?
No!! it's not going to help us get out of here!
there, there, captain asiago... don't listen to him! kernel's just being lactose intolerant
pat pat
rub rub
oh no, we've created a muenster...
AAAGHH! YOU GAVE IT A NAME?!!
damian

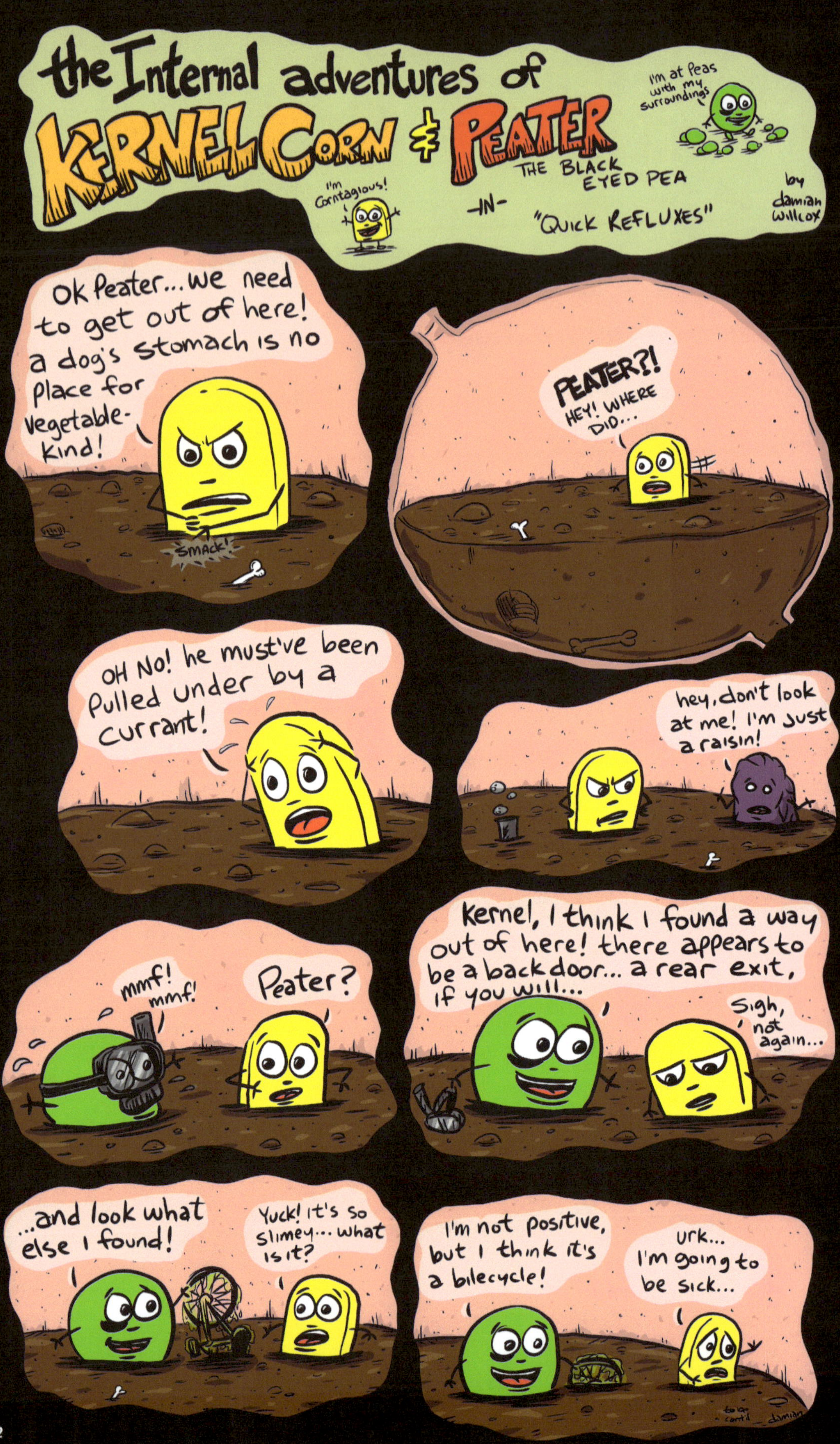
the Internal adventures of
KERNEL CORN & PEATER
THE BLACK EYED PEA
I'm at Peas with my surroundings
I'm Corntagious!
-IN-
"QUICK REFLUXES"
by damian willcox
Ok Peater... we need to get out of here! a dog's stomach is no place for vegetable-kind!
SMACK!
PEATER?! HEY! WHERE DID...
OH No! he must've been pulled under by a currant!
hey, don't look at me! I'm just a raisin!
mmf! mmf!
Peater?
Kernel, I think I found a way out of here! there appears to be a back door... a rear exit, if you will...
Sigh, not again...
...and look what else I found!
Yuck! it's so slimey... what is it?
I'm not positive, but I think it's a bilecycle!
urk... I'm going to be sick...
to be cont'd
damian

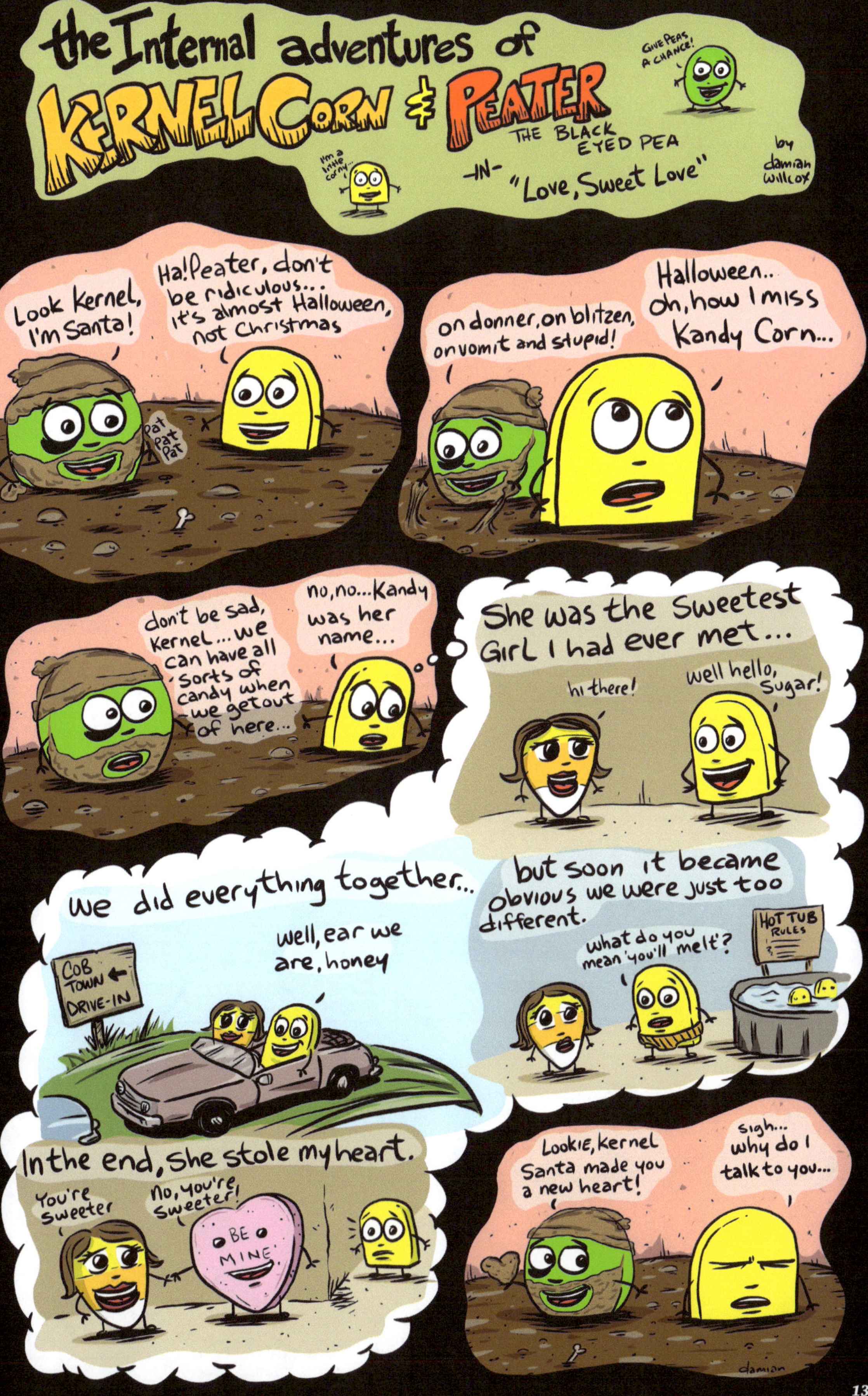
the Internal adventures of
KERNEL CORN & PEATER THE BLACK EYED PEA
Give Peas a chance!
I'm a little corny...
-IN- "Love, Sweet Love"
by damian willcox
Look Kernel, I'm Santa!
Ha! Peater, don't be ridiculous... it's almost Halloween, not Christmas
pat pat pat
on donner, on blitzen, on vomit and stupid!
Halloween.. oh, how I miss Kandy Corn...
don't be sad, Kernel... we can have all sorts of candy when we get out of here...
no, no... Kandy was her name...
She was the Sweetest Girl I had ever met...
hi there!
well hello, sugar!
We did everything together...
well, ear we are, honey
COB TOWN DRIVE-IN
but soon it became obvious we were just too different.
what do you mean 'you'll melt'?
HOT TUB RULES
In the end, She stole my heart.
You're sweeter
No, you're sweeter!
BE MINE
Lookie, Kernel Santa made you a new heart!
sigh... why do I talk to you...
damian

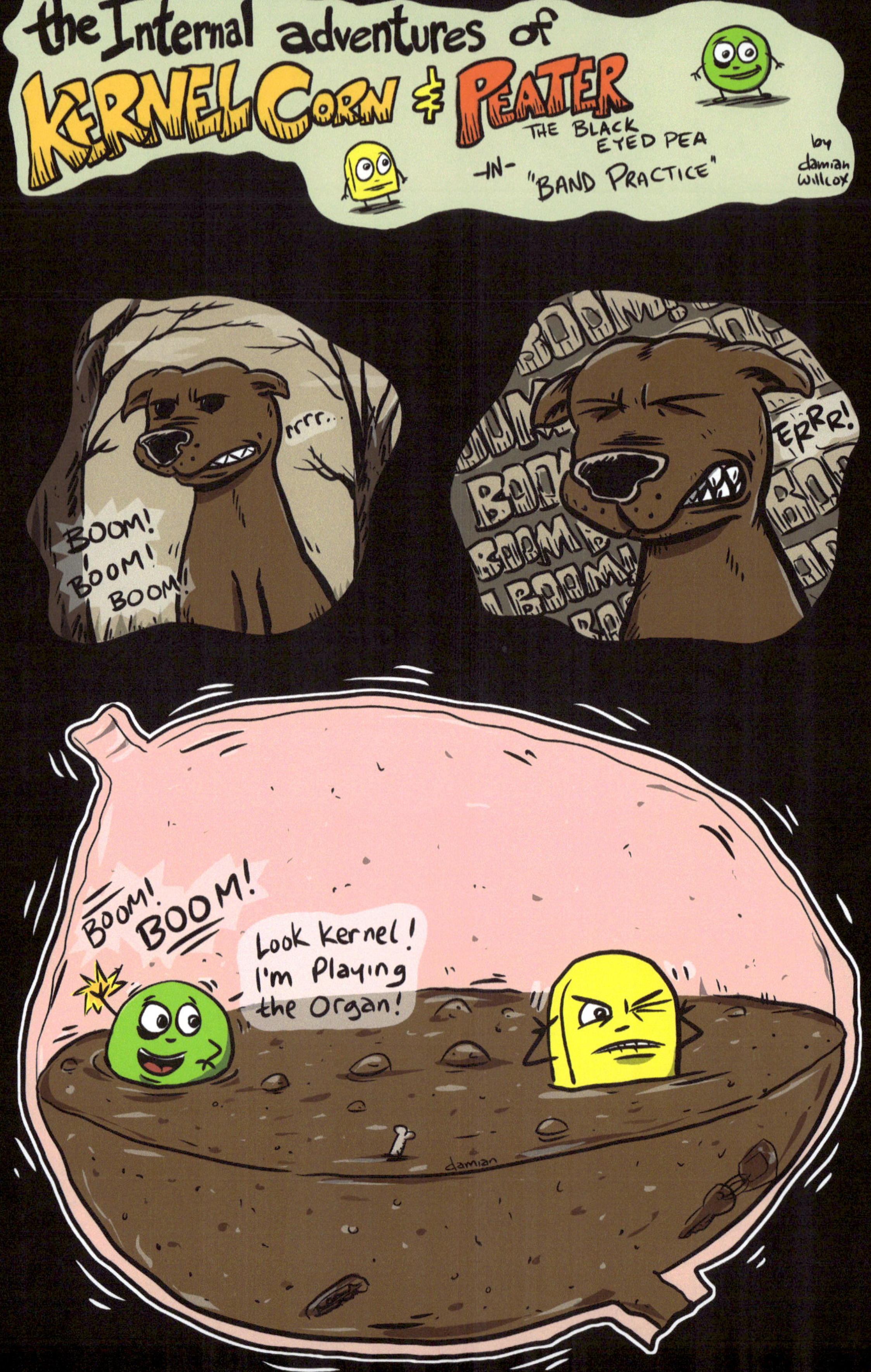
the Internal adventures of
KERNEL CORN & PEATER
THE BLACK EYED PEA
-IN- "BAND PRACTICE"
by damian willcox
rrrr..
BOOM! BOOM! BOOM!
ERRR!
BOOM! BOOM!
Look kernel! I'm Playing the Organ!
damian

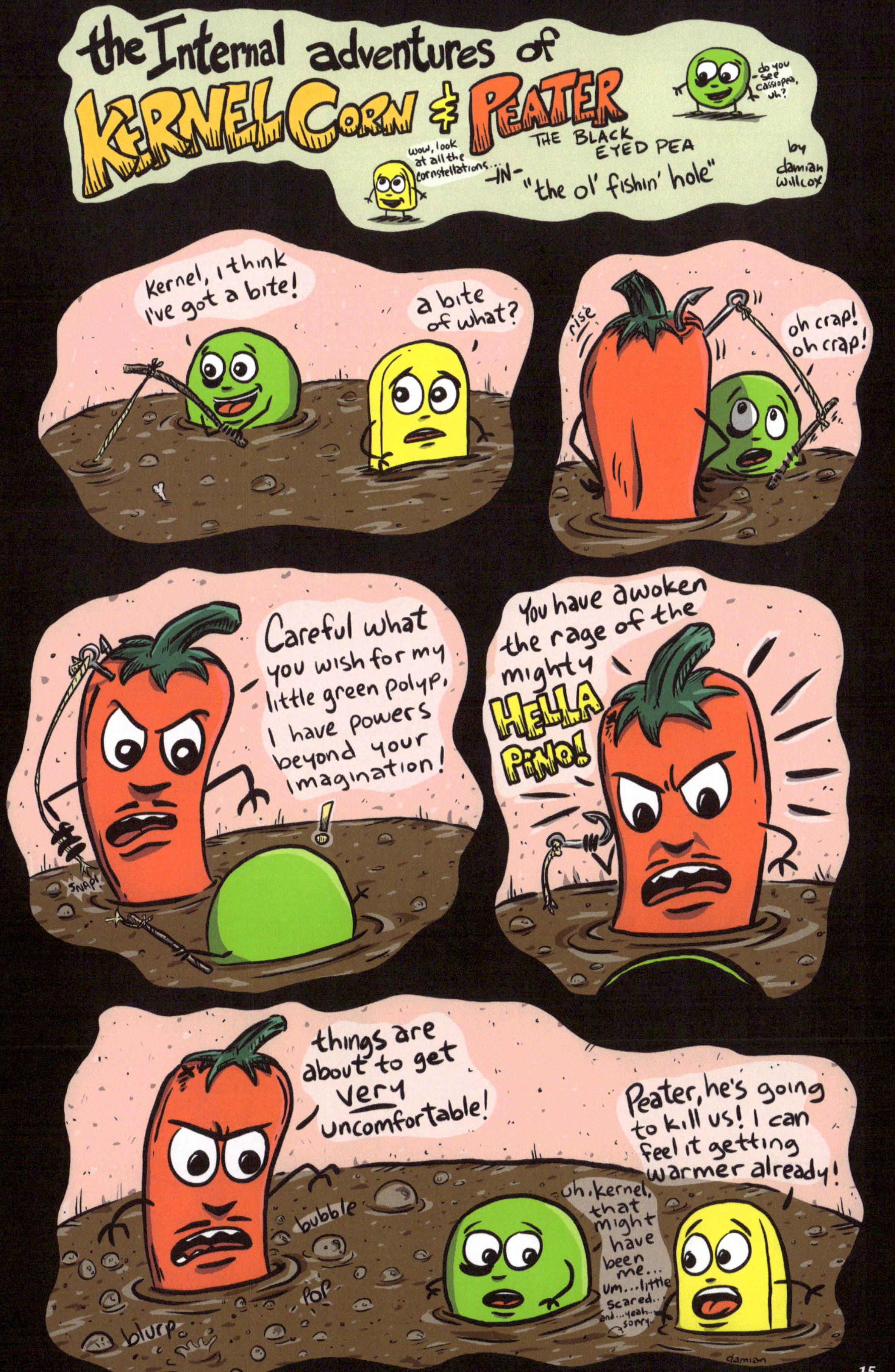
the Internal adventures of
KERNEL CORN & PEATER THE BLACK EYED PEA
do you see cassiopea, uh?
wow, look at all the constellations...
-IN- "the ol' fishin' hole"
by damian willcox
Kernel, I think I've got a bite!
a bite of what?
rise
oh crap! oh crap!
Careful what you wish for my little green polyp, I have powers beyond your imagination!
SNAP!
!
You have awoken the rage of the mighty HELLA PINO!
things are about to get very uncomfortable!
Peater, he's going to kill us! I can feel it getting warmer already!
uh, kernel, that might have been me... um...little scared... and...yeah.. sorry..
bubble
pop
blurp
damian

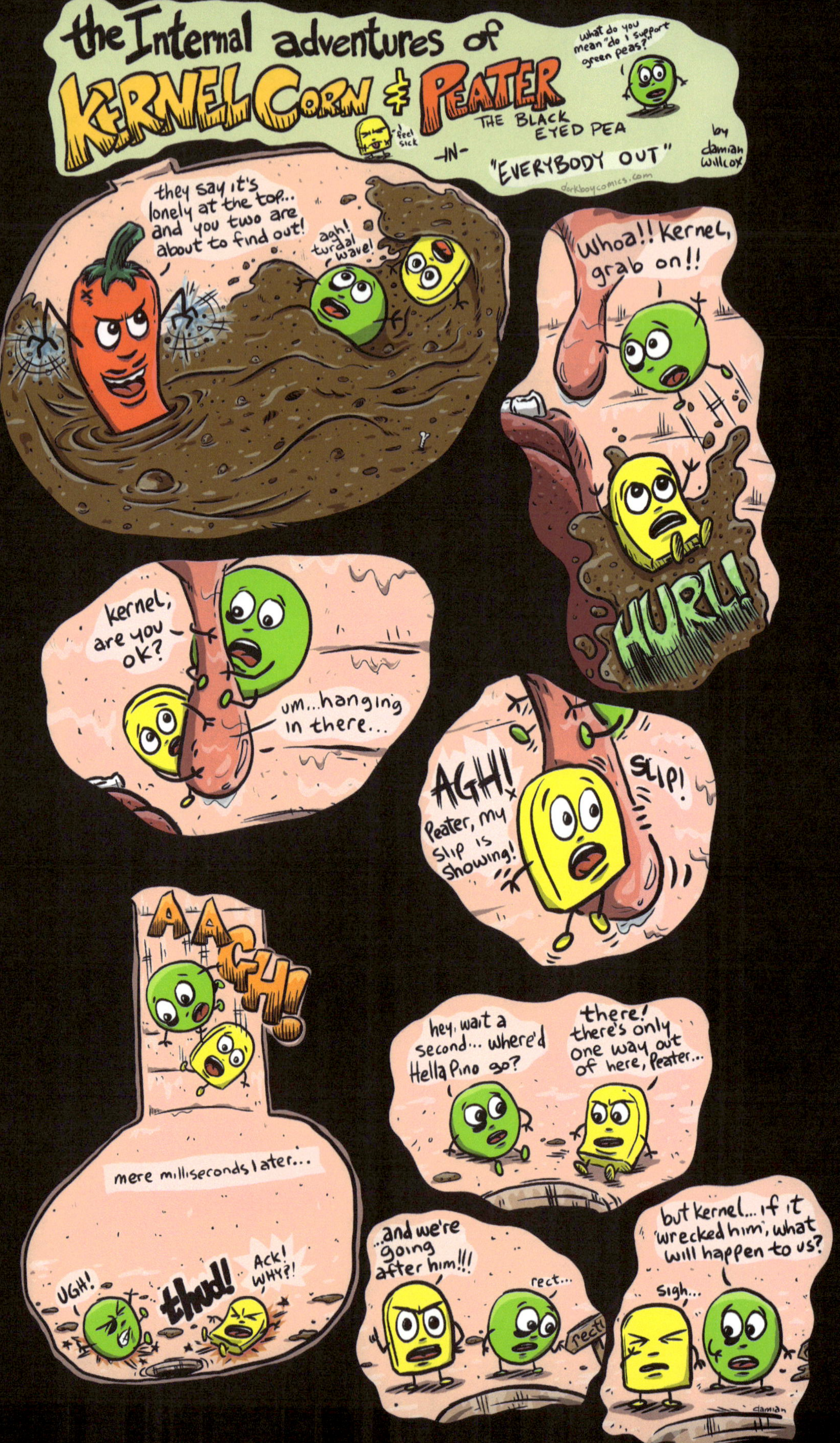

the Internal adventures of
KERNEL CORN & PEATER
THE BLACK EYED PEA
i feel sick
what do you mean "do I support green peas?"
-IN-
"EVERYBODY OUT"
by damian willcox
dorkboycomics.com
they say it's lonely at the top... and you two are about to find out!
agh! turdal wave!
Whoa!! kernel, grab on!!
HURL!
kernel, are you ok?
um...hanging in there...
AGH!
Peater, my slip is showing!
SLIP!
AACH!
mere milliseconds later...
UGH!
thud!
ACK! WHY?!
hey, wait a second... where'd Hella Pino go?
there! there's only one way out of here, Peater...
...and we're going after him!!!
rect...
rect
but kernel... if it wrecked him, what will happen to us?
sigh...
damian

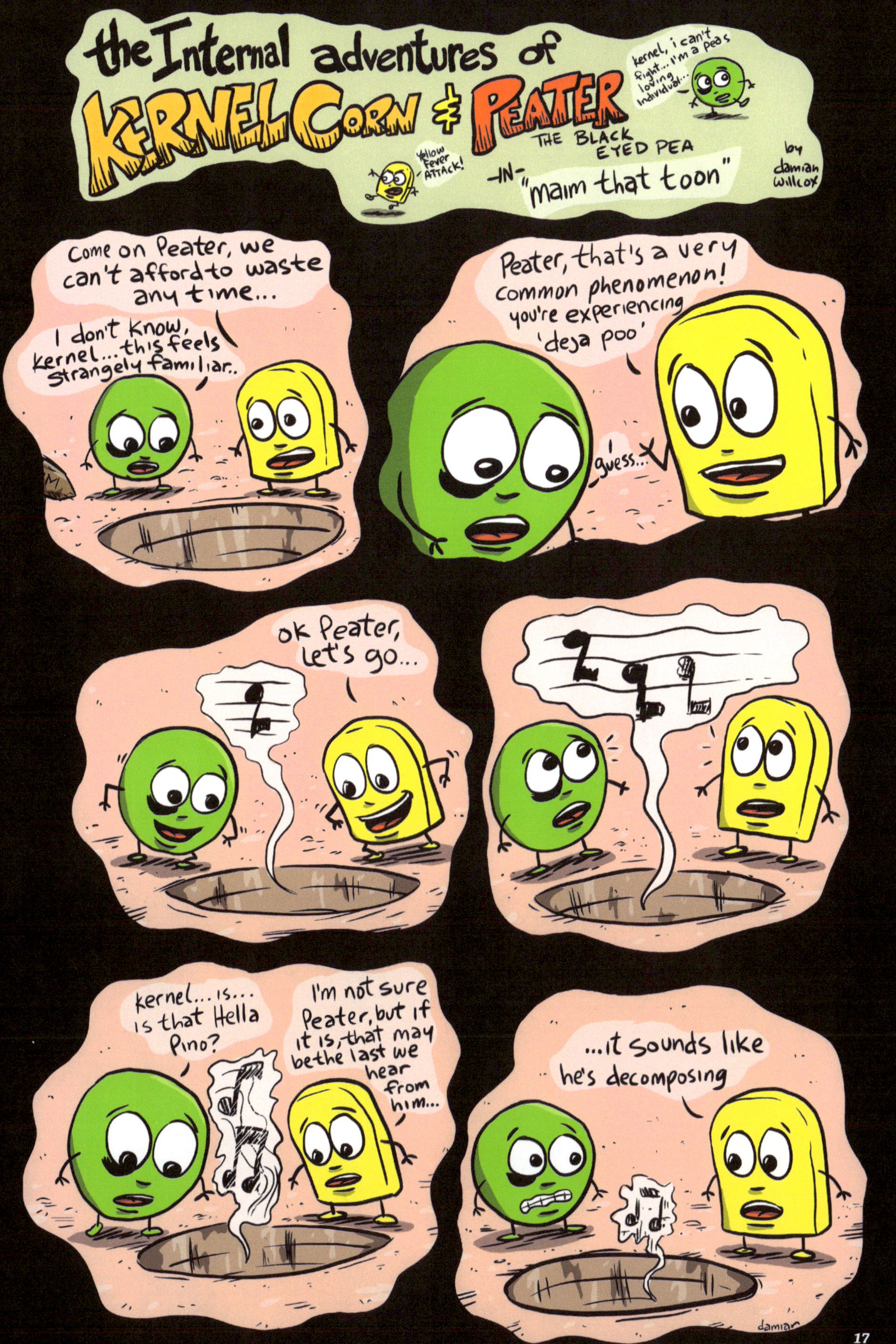

the Internal adventures of
KERNEL CORN & PEATER THE BLACK EYED PEA
kernel, i can't fight... I'm a peas loving individual...
yellow fever ATTACK!
-IN- "maim that toon"
by damian willcox
Come on Peater, we can't afford to waste any time...
I don't know, kernel... this feels strangely familiar..
Peater, that's a very common phenomenon! you're experiencing 'deja poo'
guess..
ok Peater, let's go...
kernel... is... is that Hella Pino?
I'm not sure Peater, but if it is, that may be the last we hear from him...
...it sounds like he's decomposing
damian

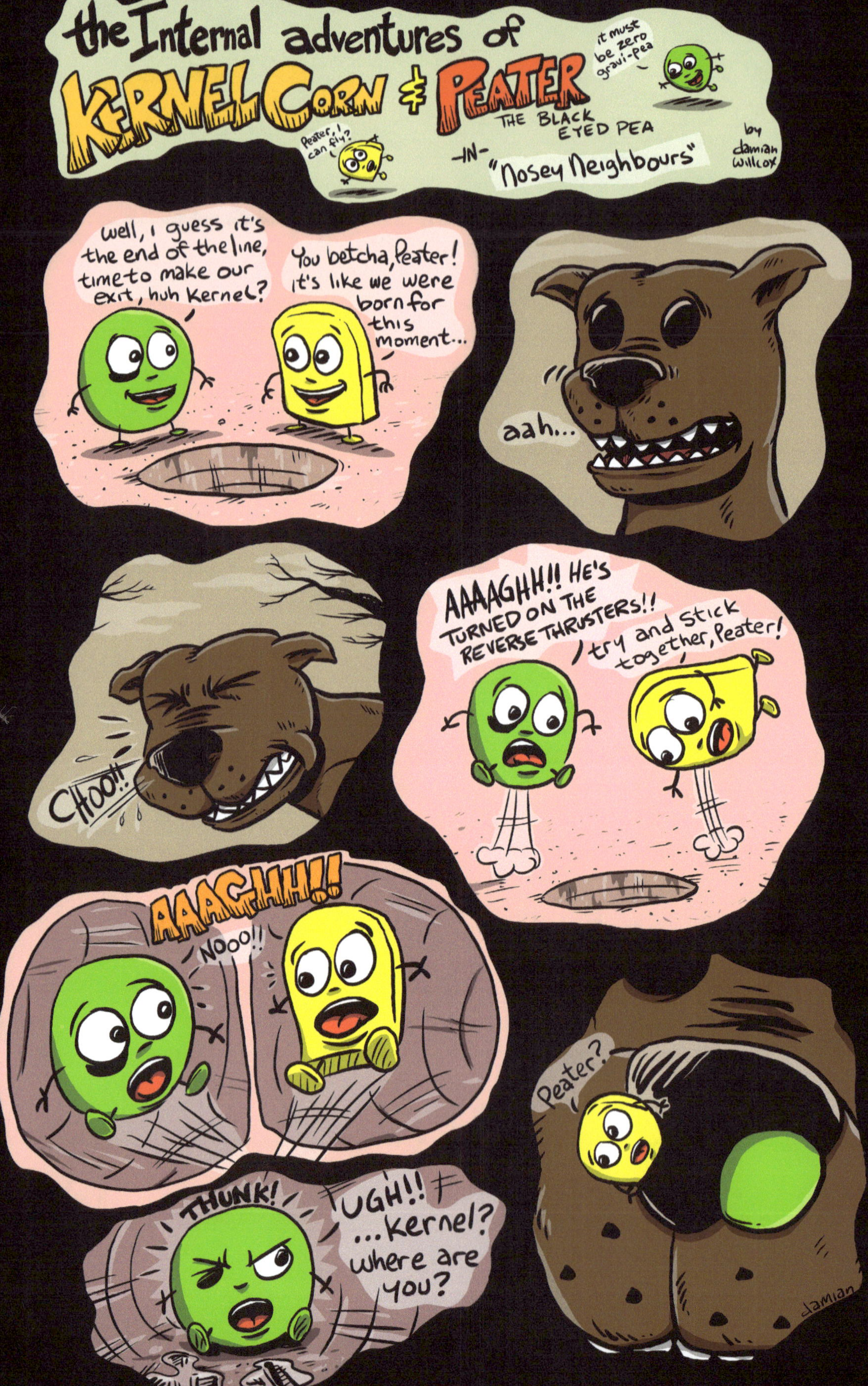
the Internal adventures of
KERNEL CORN & PEATER
THE BLACK EYED PEA
it must be zero gravi-pea
Peater, I can fly?
-IN- "Nosey Neighbours"
by damian willcox
well, I guess it's the end of the line, time to make our exit, huh Kernel?
You betcha, Peater! it's like we were born for this moment...
aah...
CHOO!!
AAAAGHH!! HE'S TURNED ON THE REVERSE THRUSTERS!!
try and stick together, Peater!
AAAGHH!!
NOOO!!
THUNK!
UGH!! ...kernel? where are you?
Peater?
damian

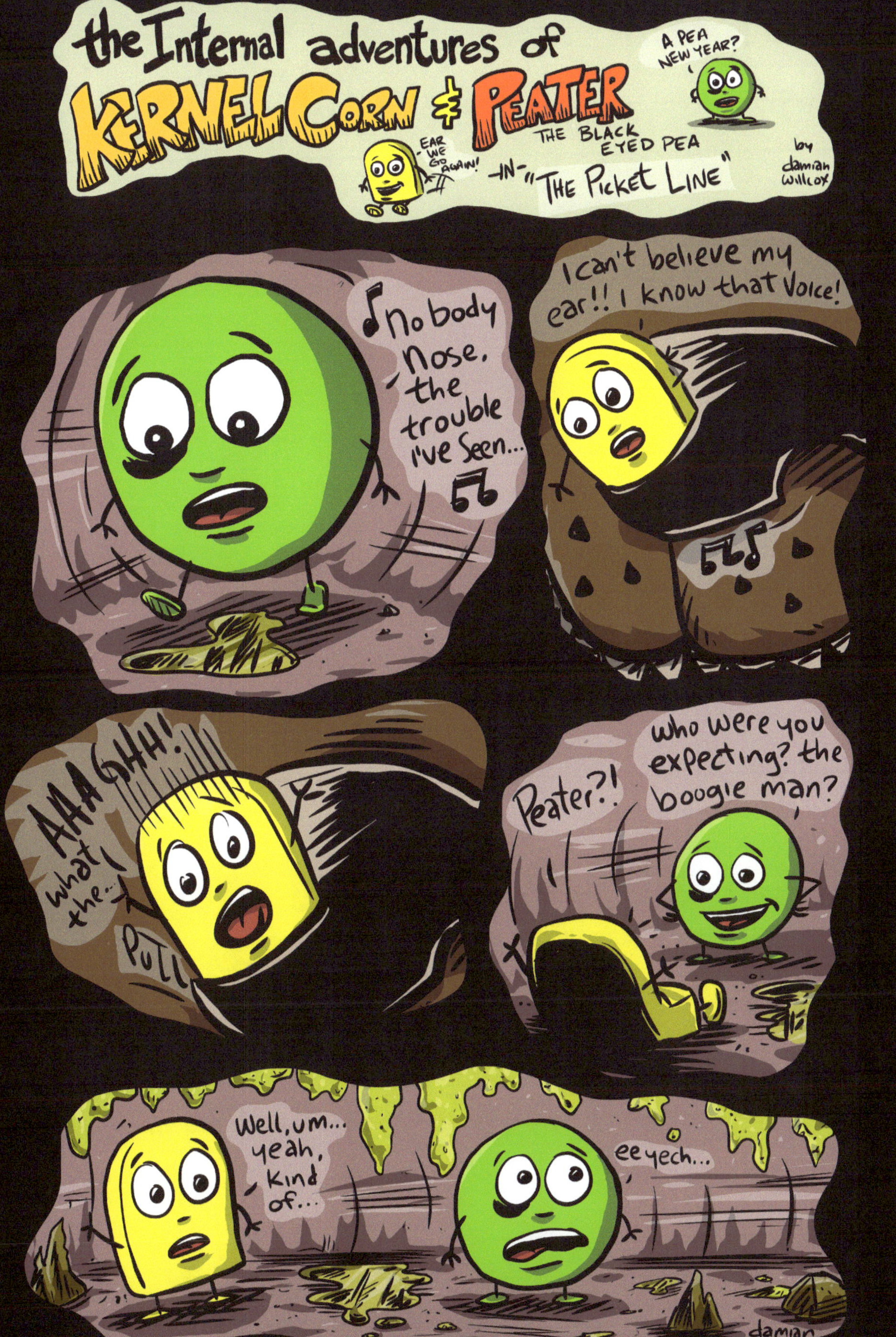
the Internal adventures of
KERNEL CORN & PEATER
THE BLACK EYED PEA
A PEA NEW YEAR?
EAR WE GO AGAIN!
-IN- "THE PICKET LINE"
by damian willcox
♪ no body nose, the trouble I've seen... ♫
I can't believe my ear!! I know that voice!
♫♪
AAAGHH!
what the...
PULL
Peater?!
who were you expecting? the boogie man?
Well, um... yeah, kind of...
ee yech...
damian

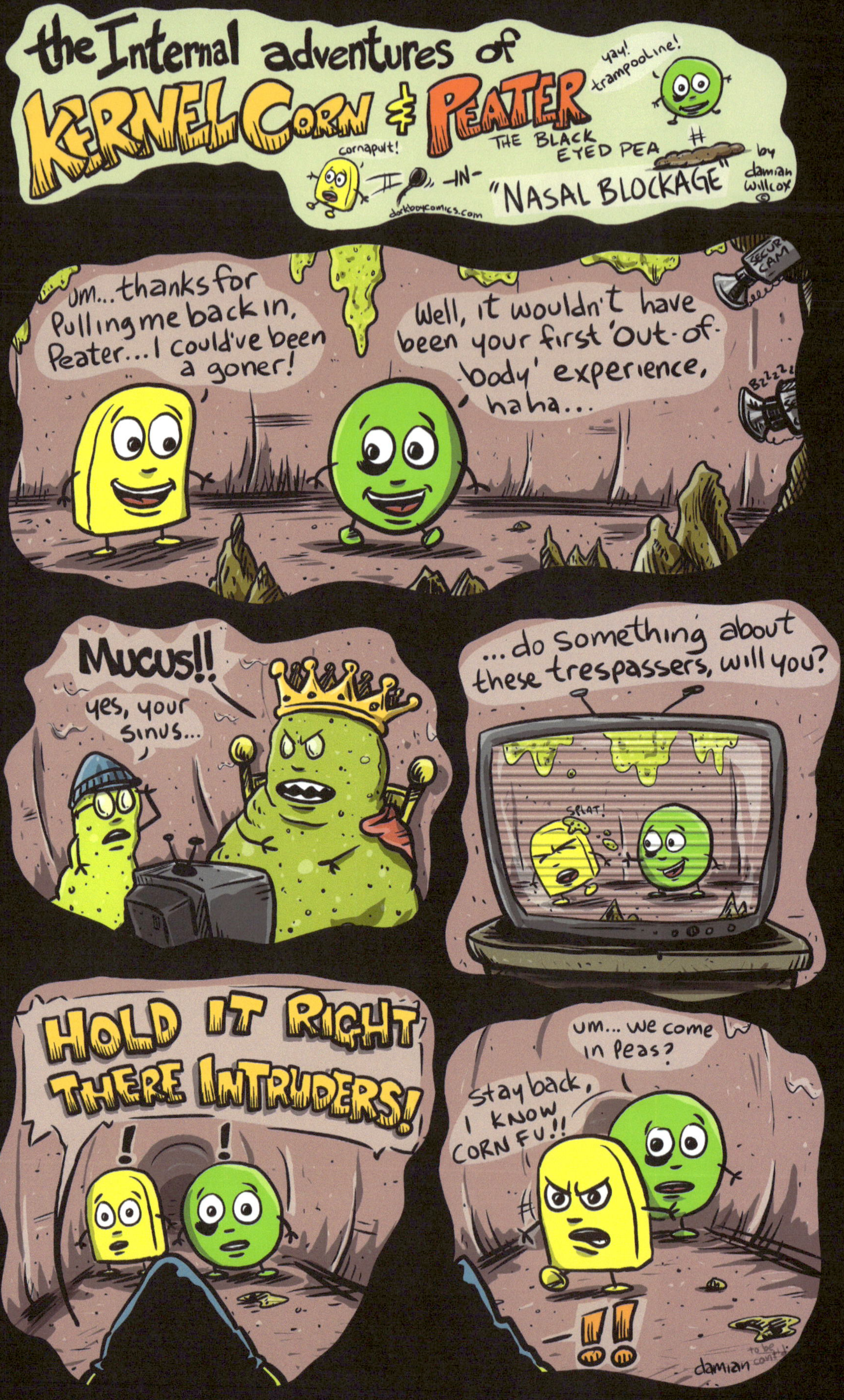

the Internal adventures of
KERNEL CORN & PEATER
THE BLACK EYED PEA
yay! trampooLine!
cornapult!
-IN-
"NASAL BLOCKAGE"
by damian willcox ©
dorkboycomics.com
SECUR CAM
um... thanks for Pulling me back in, Peater... I could've been a goner!
Well, it wouldn't have been your first 'out-of-body' experience, haha...
BZZZZ
MUCUS!!
yes, your sinus...
...do something about these trespassers, will you?
SPLAT!
HOLD IT RIGHT THERE INTRUDERS!
!
!
um... we come in Peas?
Stay back, I KNOW CORN FU!!
!!
damian
to be cont'd

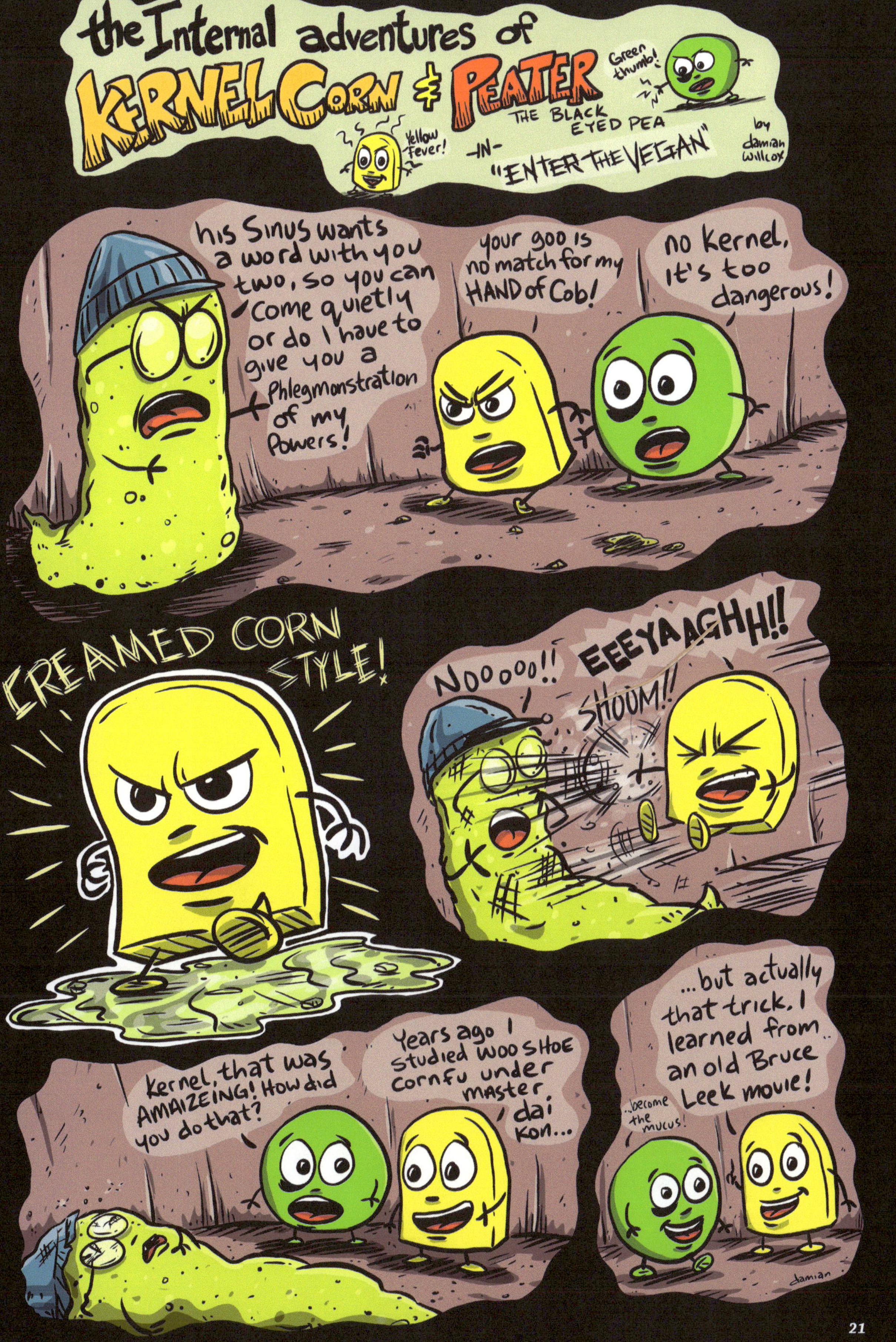
the Internal adventures of
KERNEL CORN & PEATER
THE BLACK EYED PEA
Green thumb!
Yellow fever!
-IN-
"ENTER THE VEGAN"
by damian willcox
his Sinus wants a word with you two, so you can come quietly or do I have to give you a Phlegmonstration of my Powers!
your goo is no match for my HAND of Cob!
no kernel, it's too dangerous!
CREAMED CORN STYLE!
Nooooo!!
EEEYAAGHH!!
SHOOM!!
Kernel, that was AMAIZEING! How did you do that?
Years ago I studied WOO SHOE cornfu under master dai kon...
...but actually that trick I learned from an old Bruce Leek movie!
...become the mucus!
damian

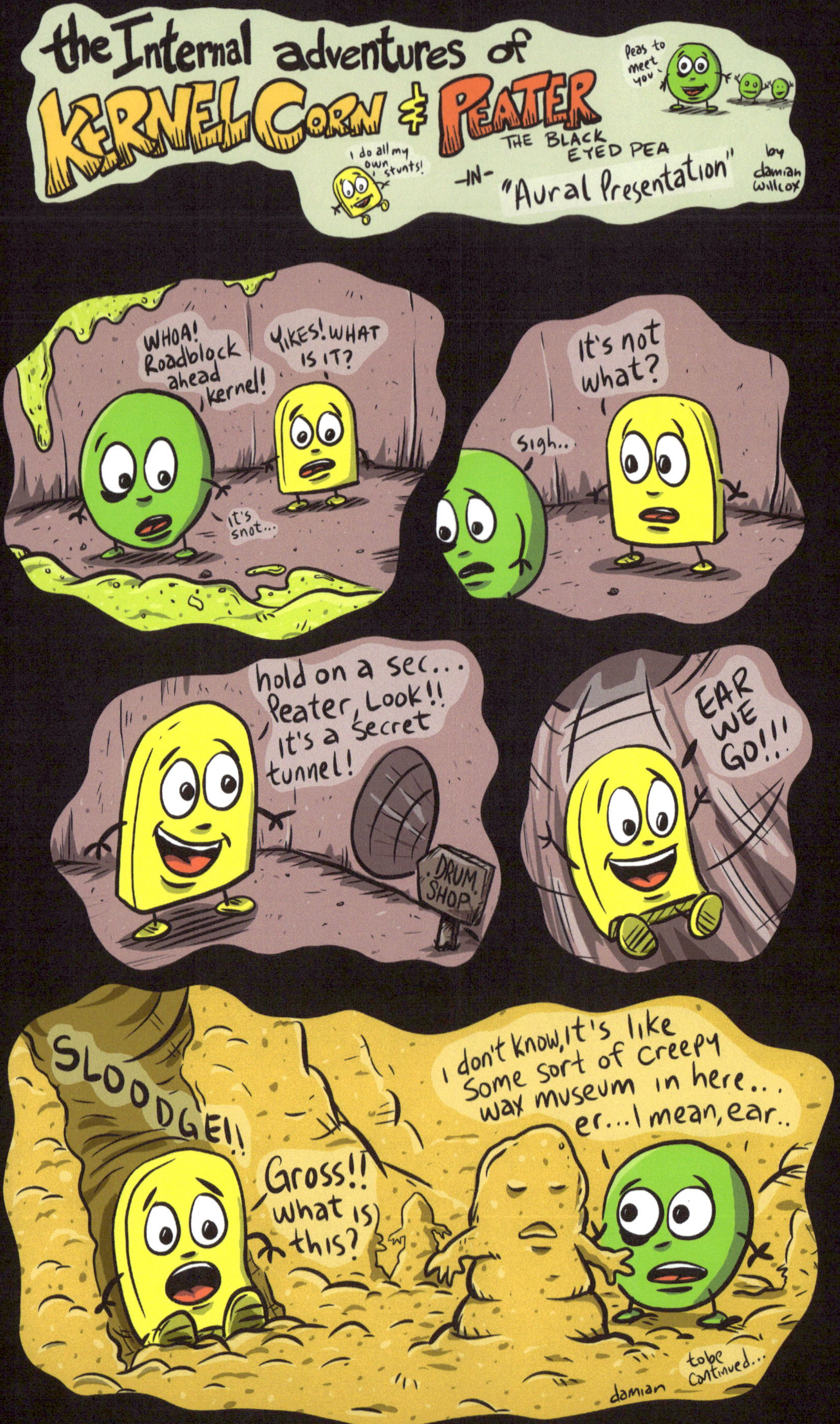
the Internal adventures of
KERNEL CORN & PEATER
THE BLACK EYED PEA
Peas to meet you.
I do all my own stunts!
-IN- "Aural Presentation"
by damian willcox
WHOA! Roadblock ahead kernel!
YIKES! WHAT IS IT?
it's snot...
It's not what?
Sigh...
hold on a sec... Peater, Look!! It's a secret tunnel!
DRUM SHOP
EAR WE GO!!!
SLOODGE!!
Gross!! what is this?
I don't know, It's like some sort of creepy wax museum in here... er...I mean, ear..
damian
tobe continued...

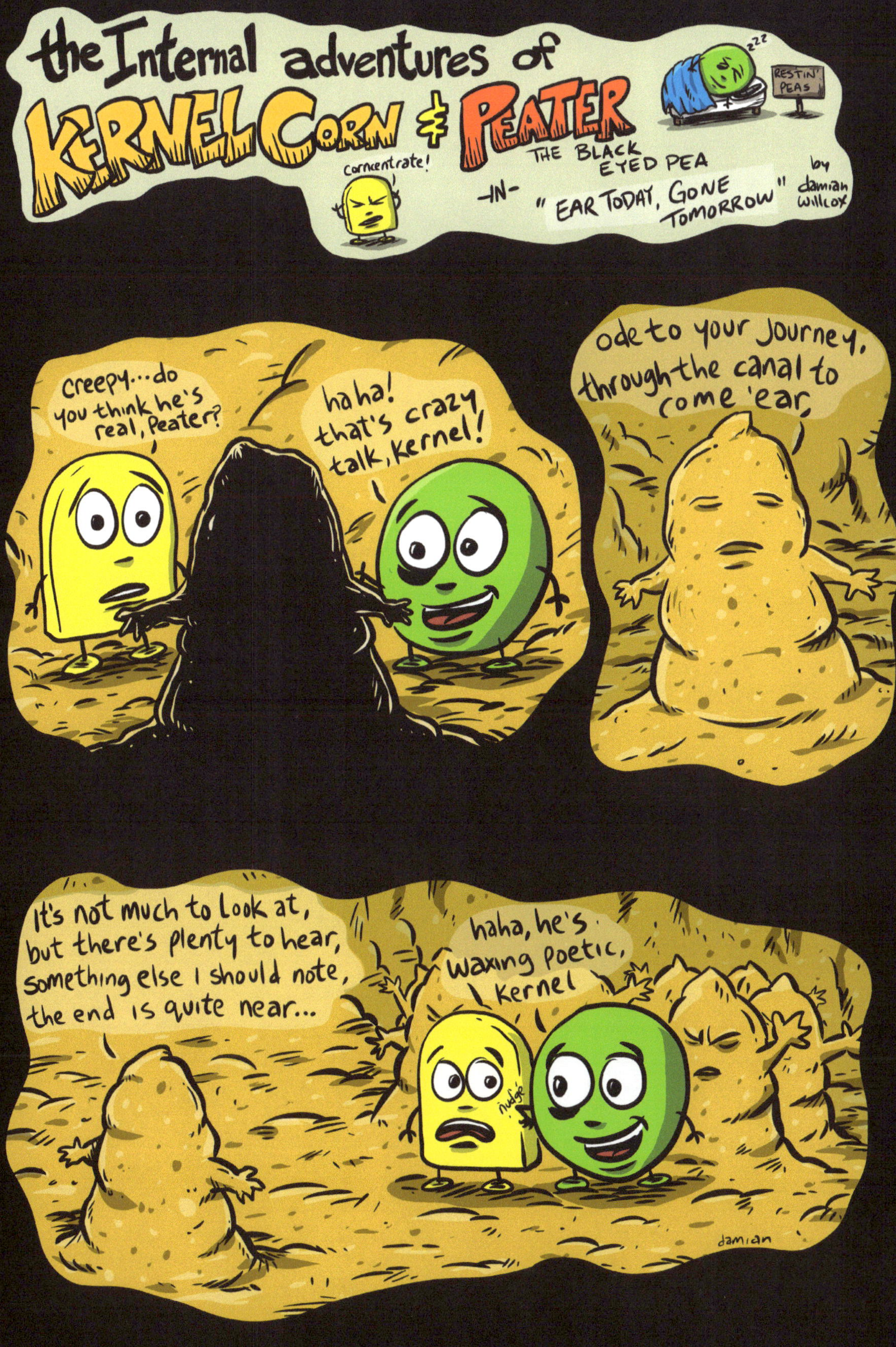
the Internal adventures of
KERNEL CORN & PEATER
THE BLACK EYED PEA
concentrate!
RESTIN' PEAS
-IN-
"EAR TODAY, GONE TOMORROW"
by damian willcox
creepy...do you think he's real, Peater?
haha! that's crazy talk, kernel!
ode to your journey, through the canal to come 'ear,
It's not much to look at, but there's plenty to hear, something else I should note, the end is quite near...
haha, he's waxing poetic, kernel
nudge
damian

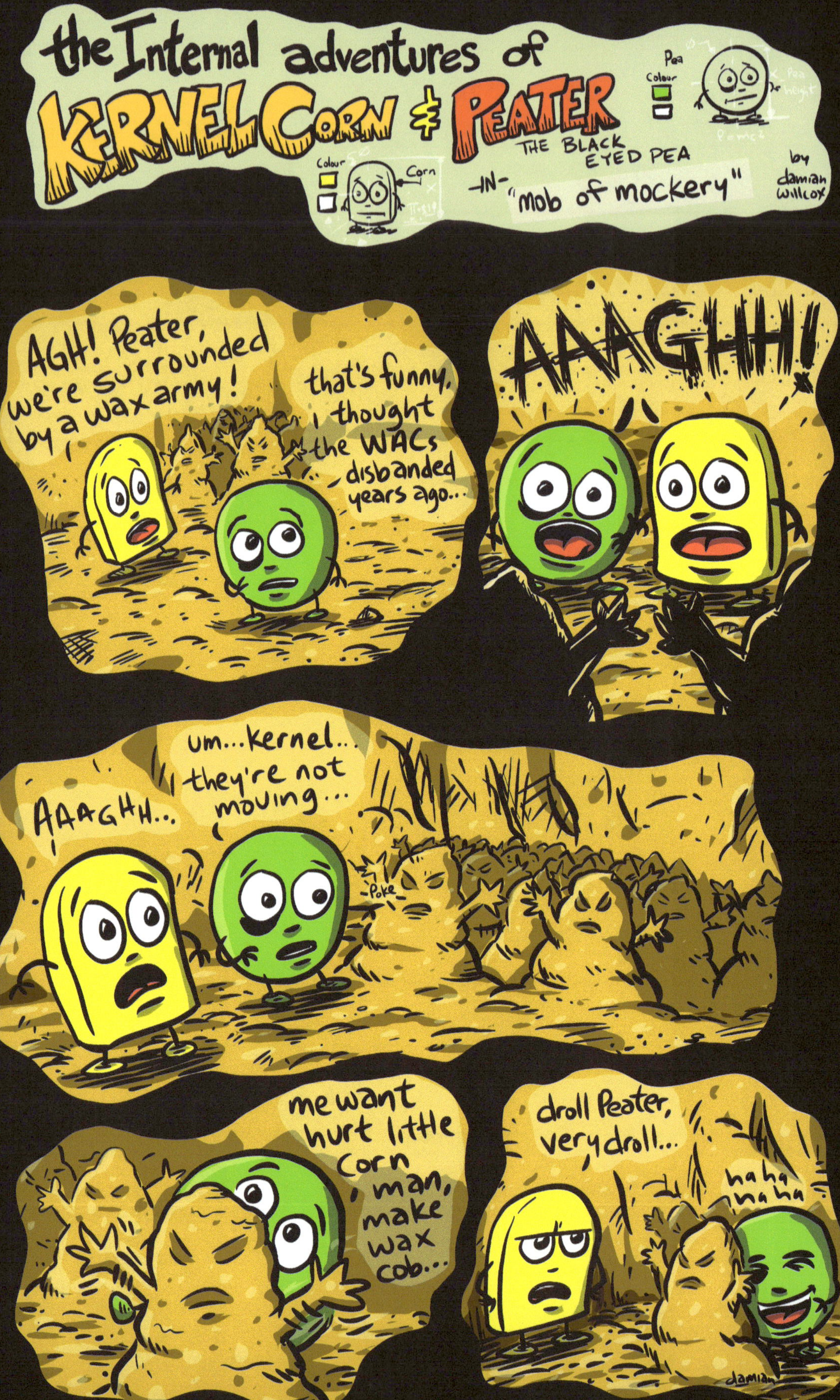
the Internal adventures of
KERNEL CORN & PEATER
THE BLACK EYED PEA
-IN- "mob of mockery"
by damian willcox
Pea
Colour
Colour
Corn
AGH! Peater, we're surrounded by a wax army!
that's funny, I thought the WACs disbanded years ago..
AAAGHH!
AAAGHH...
um...kernel.. they're not moving...
poke
me want hurt little corn man, make wax cob...
droll Peater, very droll...
ha ha ha ha
damian

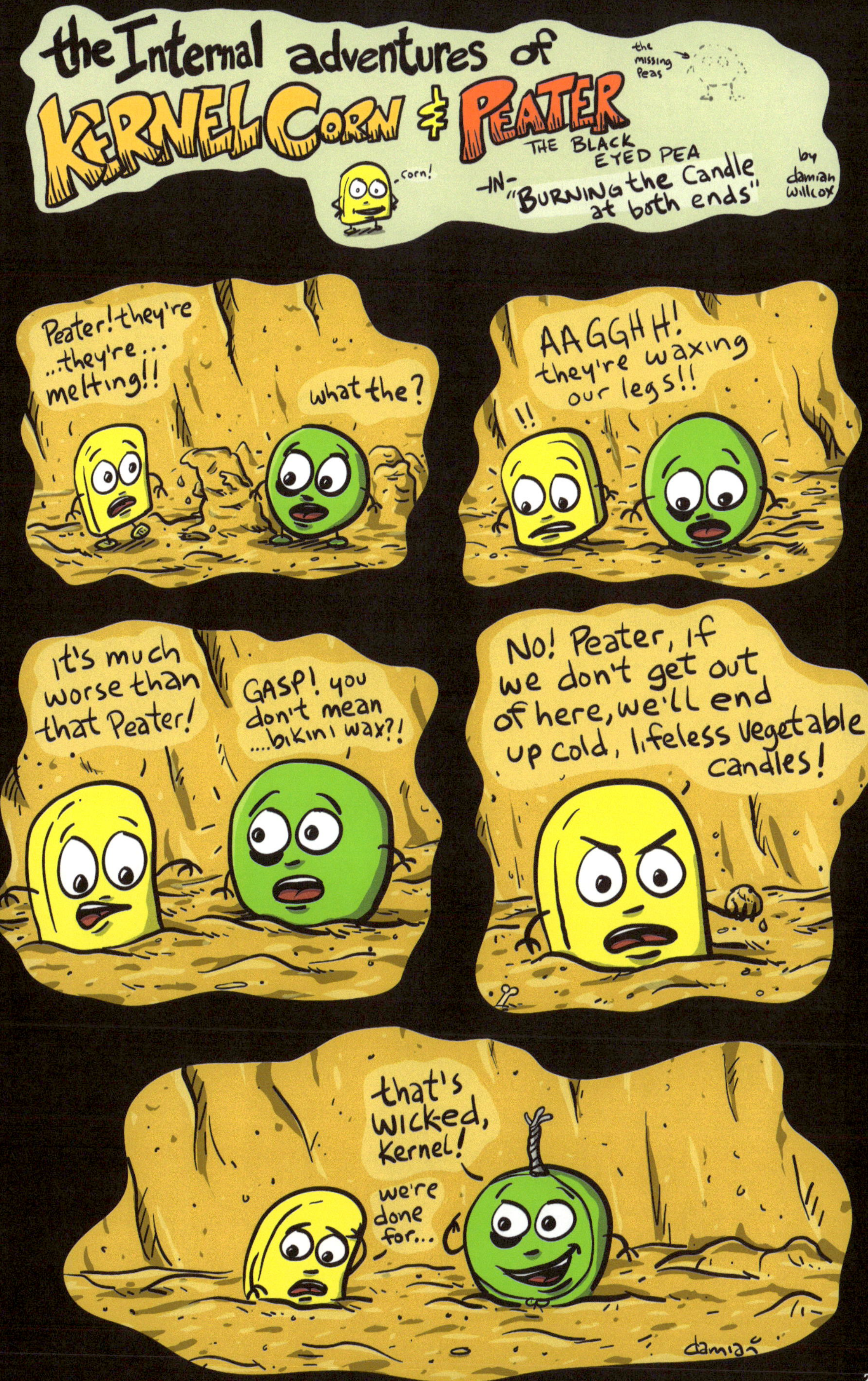

the Internal adventures of
KERNEL CORN & PEATER
THE BLACK EYED PEA
the missing Peas
-corn!
-IN- "BURNING the Candle at both ends"
by damian willcox
Peater! they're ...they're... melting!!
what the?
AAGGHH! they're waxing our legs!!
!!
It's much worse than that Peater!
GASP! you don't mean ....bikini wax?!
No! Peater, if we don't get out of here, we'll end up cold, lifeless vegetable candles!
that's wicked, Kernel!
we're done for...
damian

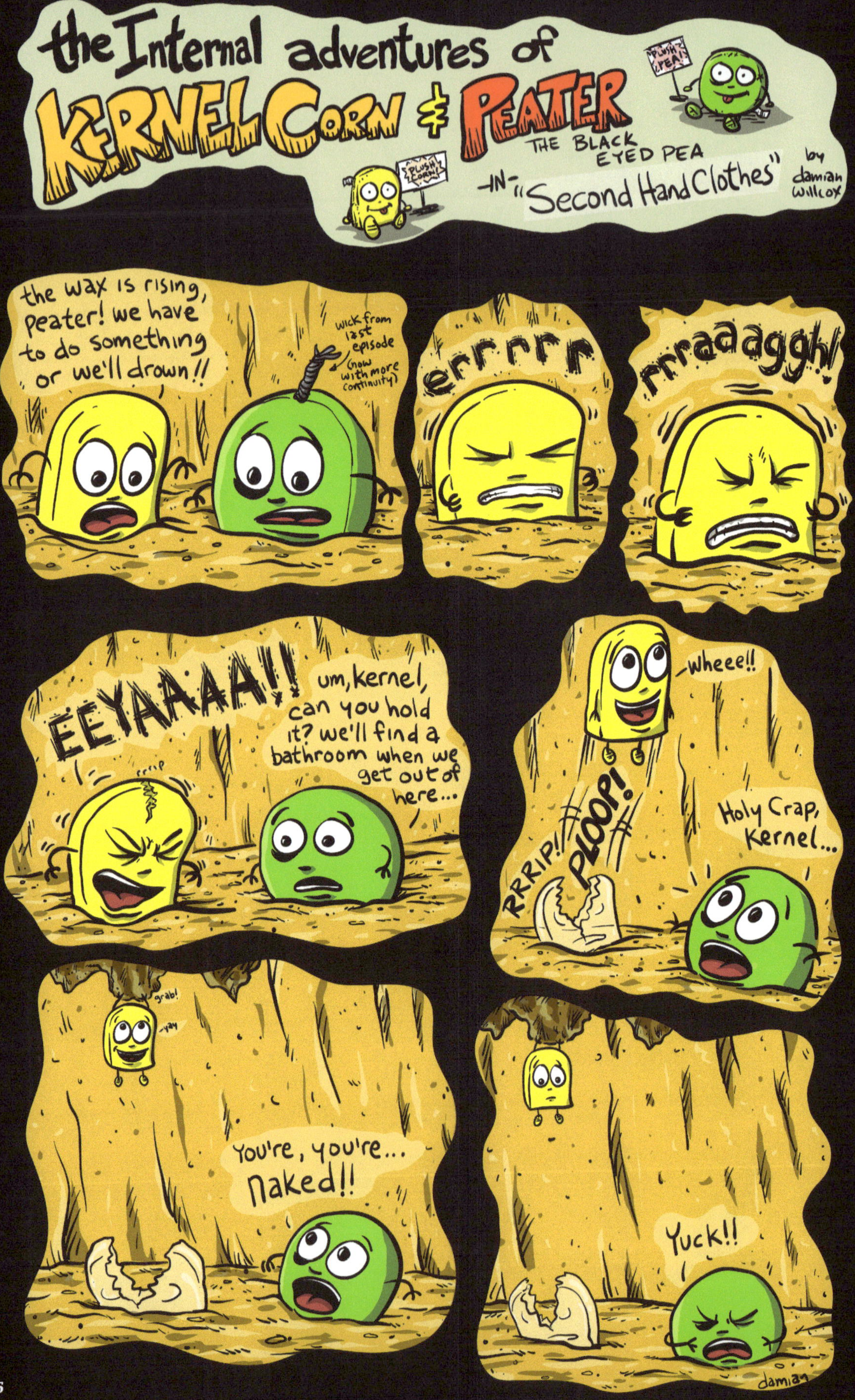

the Internal adventures of
KERNEL CORN & PEATER
THE BLACK EYED PEA
PLUSH PEA!
PLUSH CORN!
-IN- "Second Hand Clothes"
by damian willcox
the wax is rising, peater! we have to do something or we'll drown!!
wick from last episode (now with more continuity)
errrrr
rrraaaggh!
EEYAAAA!!
rrrip
um, kernel, can you hold it? we'll find a bathroom when we get out of here...
wheee!!
RRRIP!!
PLOOP!
Holy Crap, Kernel...
grab!
yay
You're, you're... naked!!
Yuck!!
damian

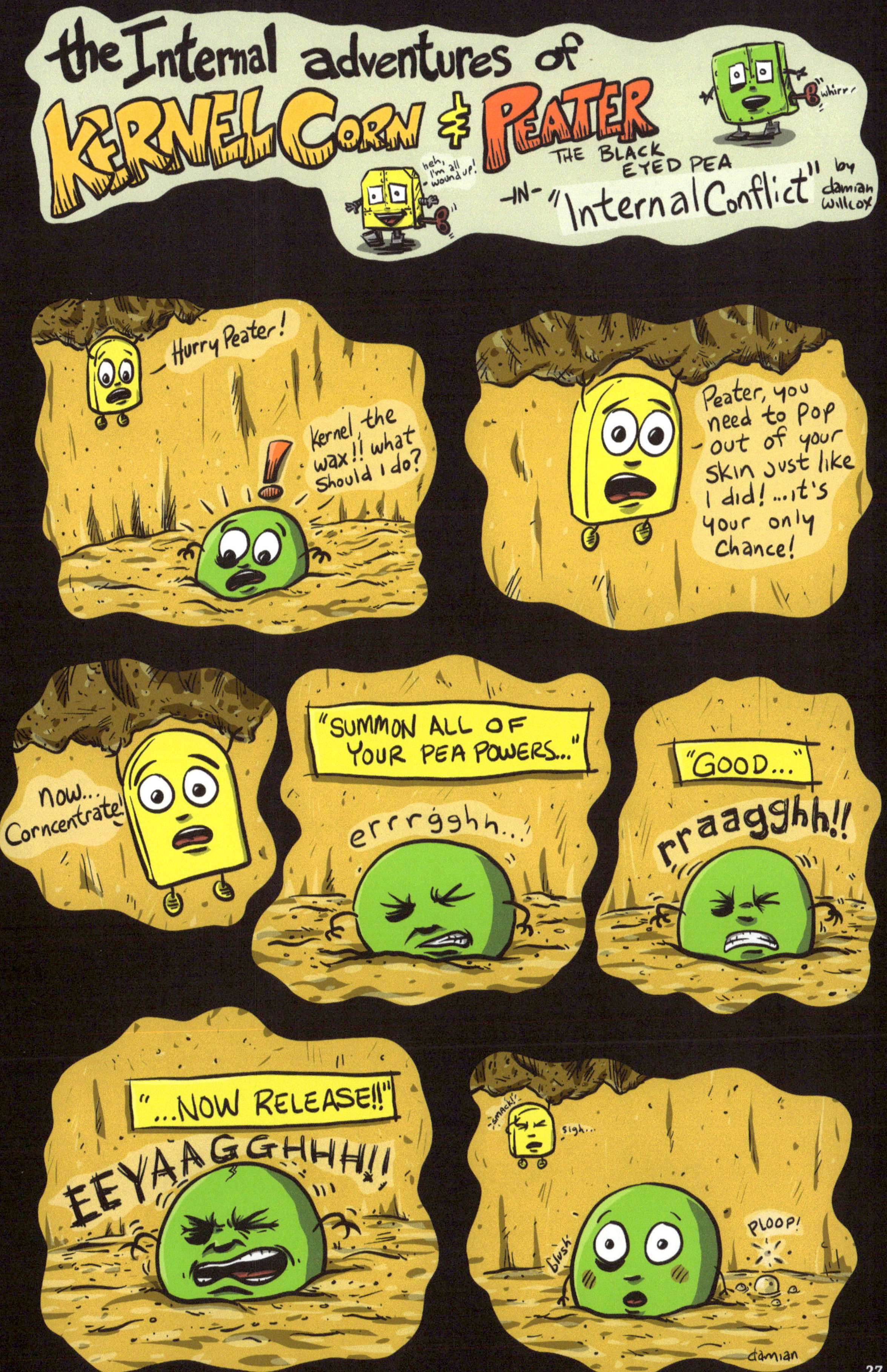
the Internal adventures of
KERNEL CORN & PEATER
THE BLACK EYED PEA
heh, I'm all wound up!
whirr
-IN- "Internal Conflict"
by damian willcox
Hurry Peater!
Kernel the wax!! what should I do?
Peater, you need to pop out of your skin just like I did! ...it's your only chance!
now... Corncentrate!
"SUMMON ALL OF YOUR PEA POWERS..."
errrgghh...
"GOOD..."
rraagghh!!
"...NOW RELEASE!!"
EEYAAGGHHH!!
smack!
sigh...
Glush
PLOOP!
damian

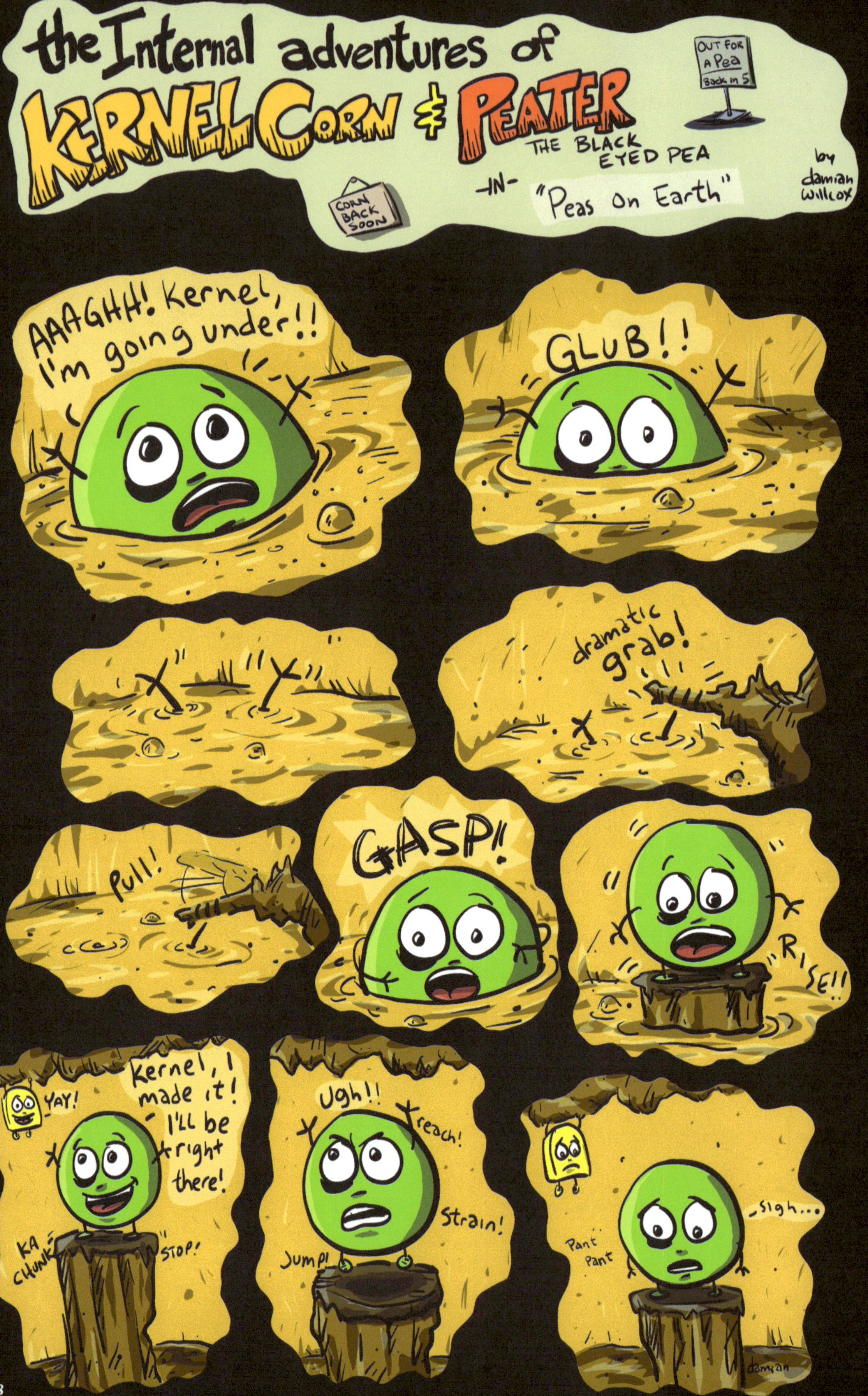
the Internal adventures of
KERNEL CORN & PEATER
THE BLACK EYED PEA
OUT FOR A Pea Back in 5
-IN-
"Peas On Earth"
CORN BACK SOON
by damian willcox
AAAGHH! Kernel, I'm going under!!
GLUB!!
dramatic grab!
Pull!
GASP!
RISE!!
YAY!
Kernel, I made it! I'll be right there!
KA CHUNK
STOP!
Ugh!!
reach!
Strain!
Jump!
Pant Pant
-sigh...
damian

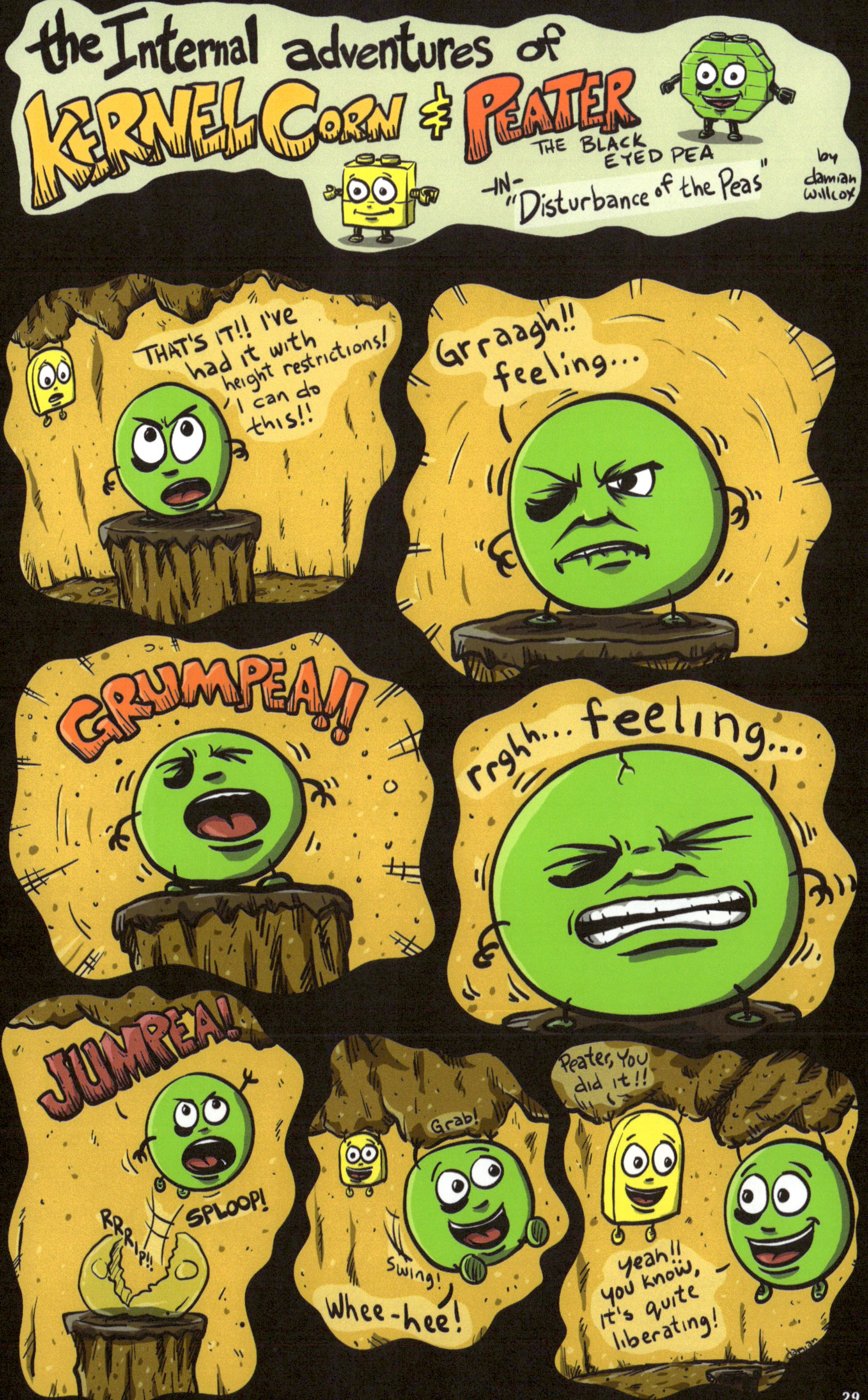
the Internal adventures of
KERNEL CORN & PEATER THE BLACK EYED PEA
-IN- "Disturbance of the Peas"
by damian willcox
THAT'S IT!! I've had it with height restrictions! I can do this!!
Grraagh!! feeling...
GRUMPEA!!
rrghh... feeling...
JUMPEA!
RRRIP!!
SPLOOP!
Grab!
Swing!
Whee-hee!
Peater, You did it!!
yeah!! you know, it's quite liberating!

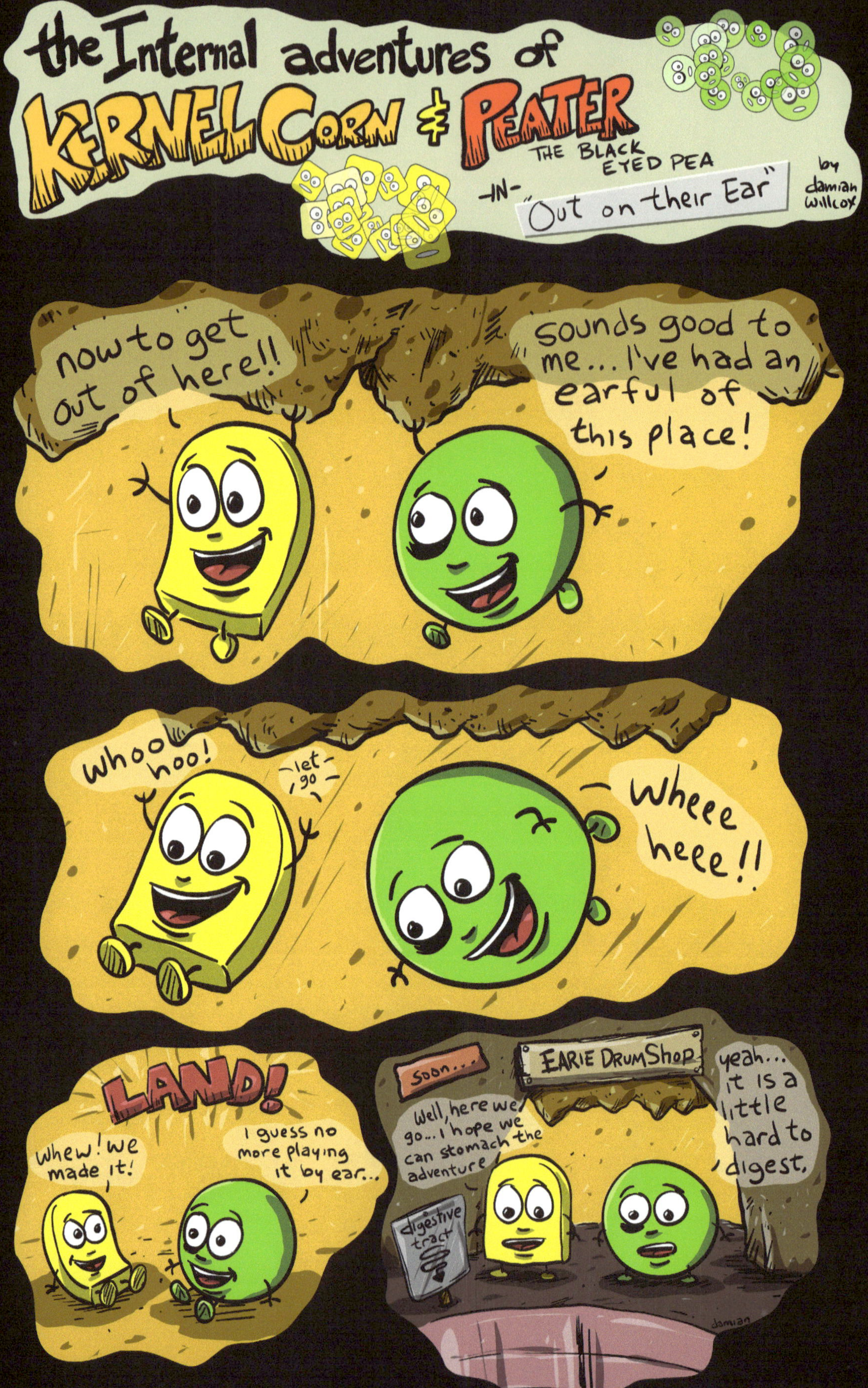

the Internal adventures of
KERNEL CORN & PEATER
THE BLACK EYED PEA
-IN- "Out on their Ear"
by damian willcox
now to get out of here!!
sounds good to me... I've had an earful of this place!
whoo hoo!
let go
wheee heee!!
LAND!
whew! we made it!
I guess no more playing it by ear...
soon...
EARIE DRUM SHOP
well, here we go... I hope we can stomach the adventure
yeah... it is a little hard to digest.
digestive tract
damian

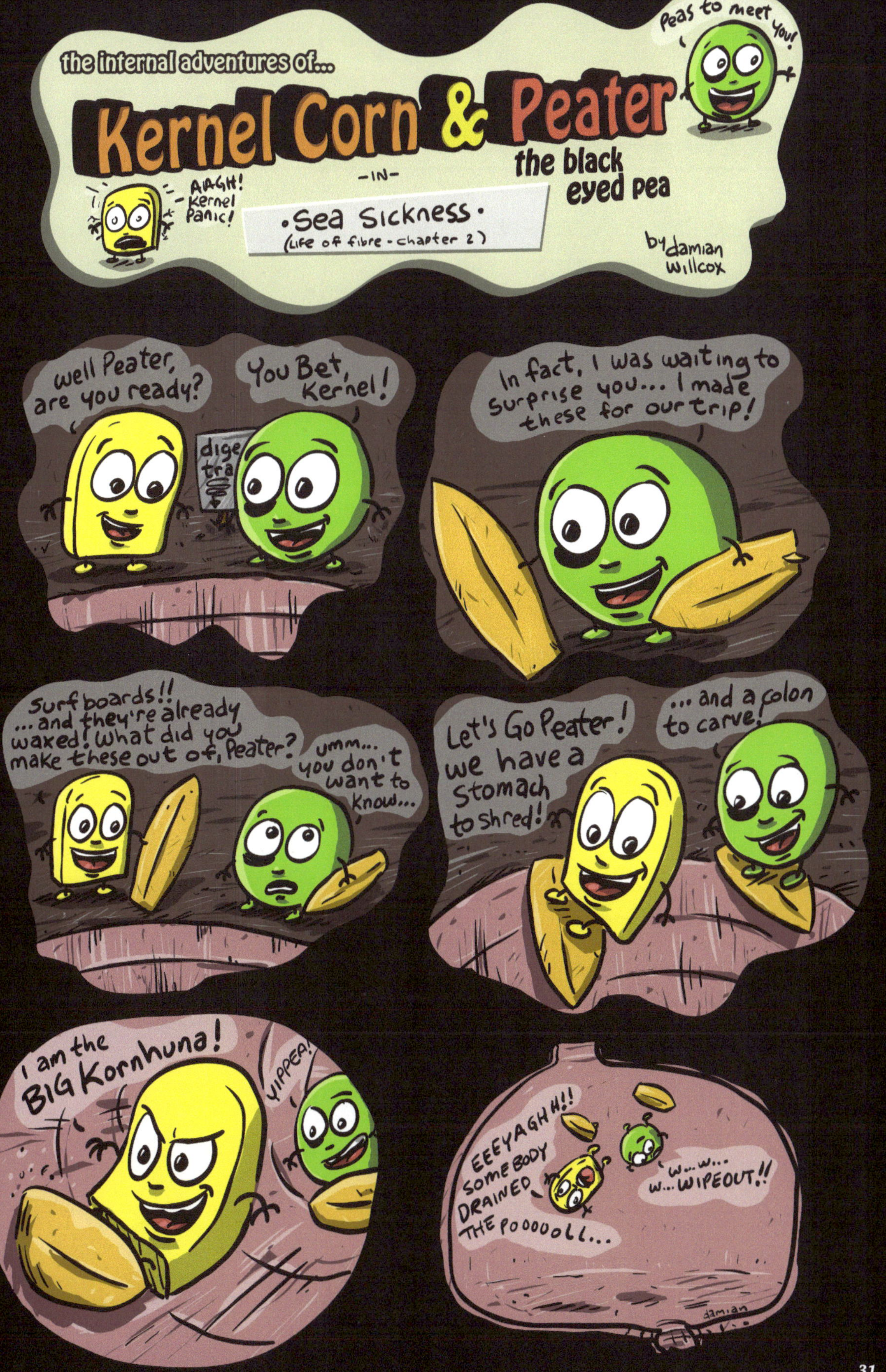
the internal adventures of...
Kernel Corn & Peater the black eyed pea
Peas to meet you!
AAGH! Kernel Panic!
-IN-
•Sea Sickness•
(Life of fibre - chapter 2)
by damian willcox
well Peater, are you ready?
You Bet, Kernel!
In fact, I was waiting to surprise you... I made these for our trip!
Surf boards!! ...and they're already waxed! What did you make these out of, Peater?
umm... you don't want to know...
Let's Go Peater! we have a Stomach to shred!
...and a colon to carve!
I am the BIG Kornhuna!
YIPPEE!
EEEYAGHH!! SOMEBODY DRAINED THE POOOOOLL...
W...W... W...WIPEOUT!!
damian

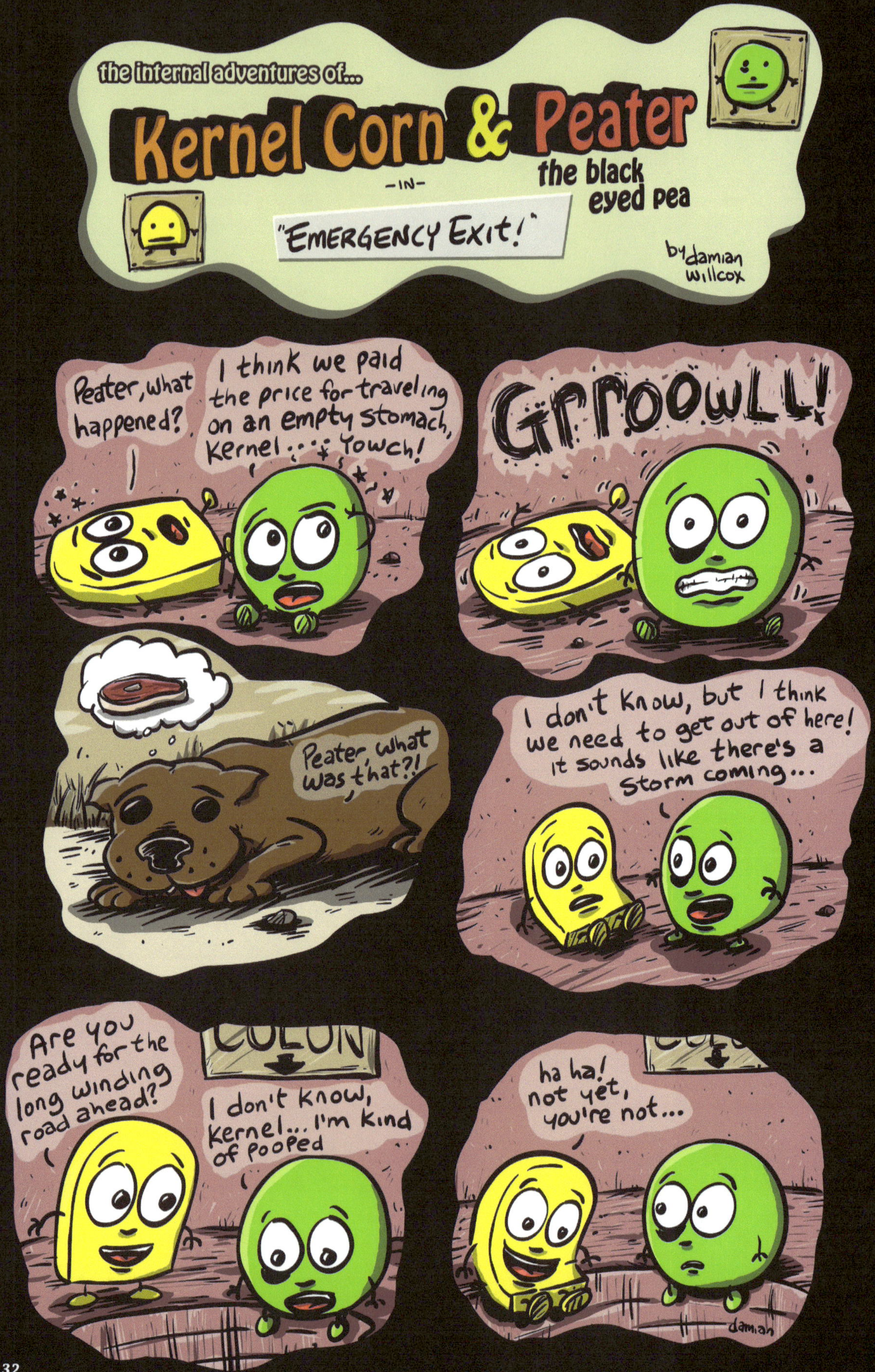

the internal adventures of...
Kernel Corn & Peater the black eyed pea
-IN-
"EMERGENCY EXIT!"
by damian willcox
Peater, what happened?
I think we paid the price for traveling on an empty stomach, Kernel... Yowch!
GRROOWLL!
Peater, what was that?!
I don't know, but I think we need to get out of here! It sounds like there's a storm coming...
Are you ready for the long winding road ahead?
COLON
I don't know, Kernel... I'm kind of pooped
ha ha! not yet, you're not...
damian

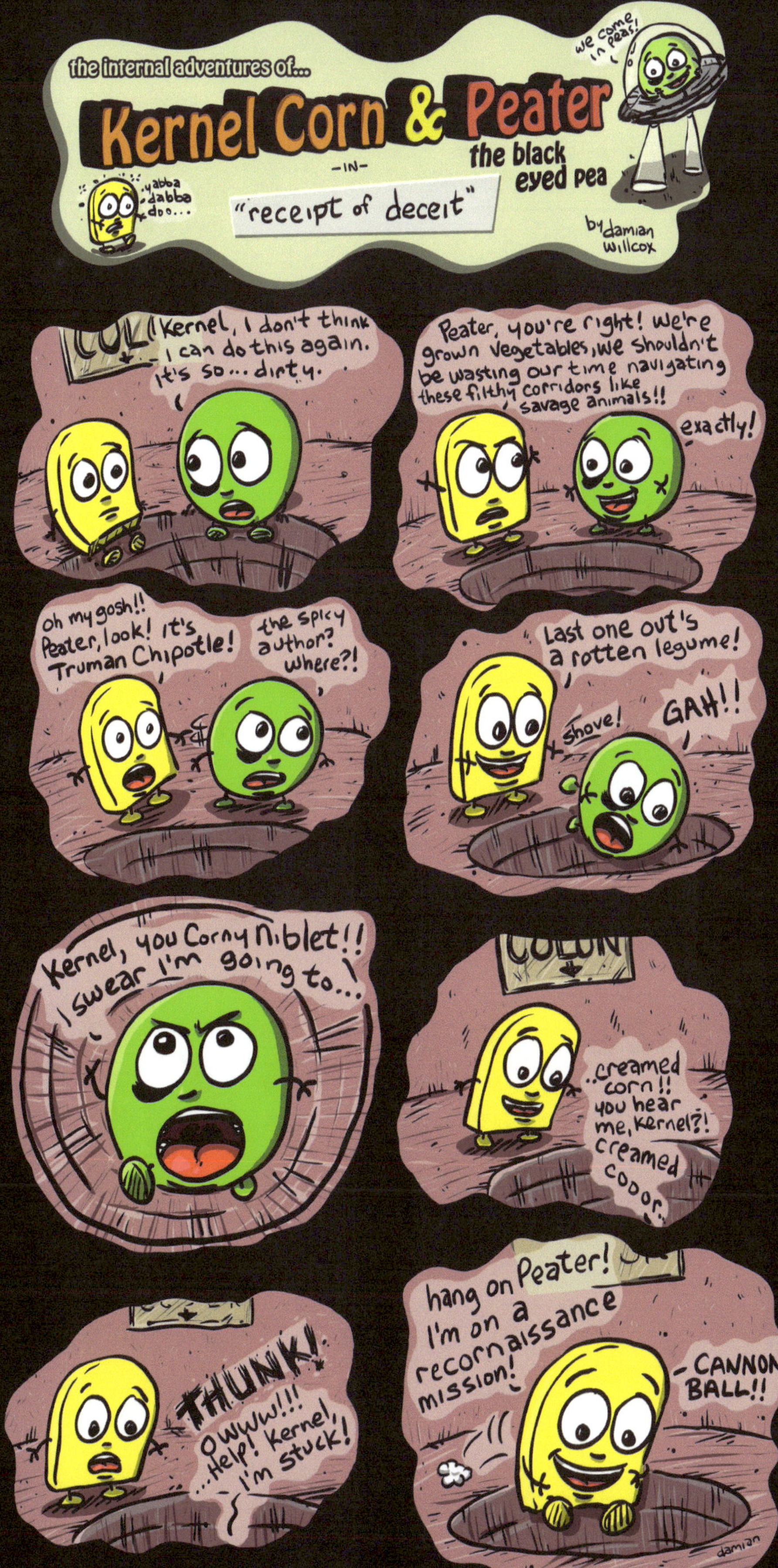

the internal adventures of...
Kernel Corn & Peater the black eyed pea
-IN-
"receipt of deceit"
by damian willcox
yabba dabba doo...
we come in peas!
Kernel, I don't think I can do this again. It's so... dirty.
Peater, you're right! We're grown vegetables, we shouldn't be wasting our time navigating these filthy corridors like savage animals!!
exactly!
oh my gosh!! Peater, look! It's Truman Chipotle!
the spicy author? where?!
Last one out's a rotten legume!
shove!
GAH!!
Kernel, you Corny niblet!! I swear I'm going to...!
COLON
...creamed corn!! you hear me, Kernel?! creamed coooor...
THUNK!
owww!!! ...Help! Kernel, I'm stuck!
hang on Peater! I'm on a reconnaissance mission!
-CANNON BALL!!
damian

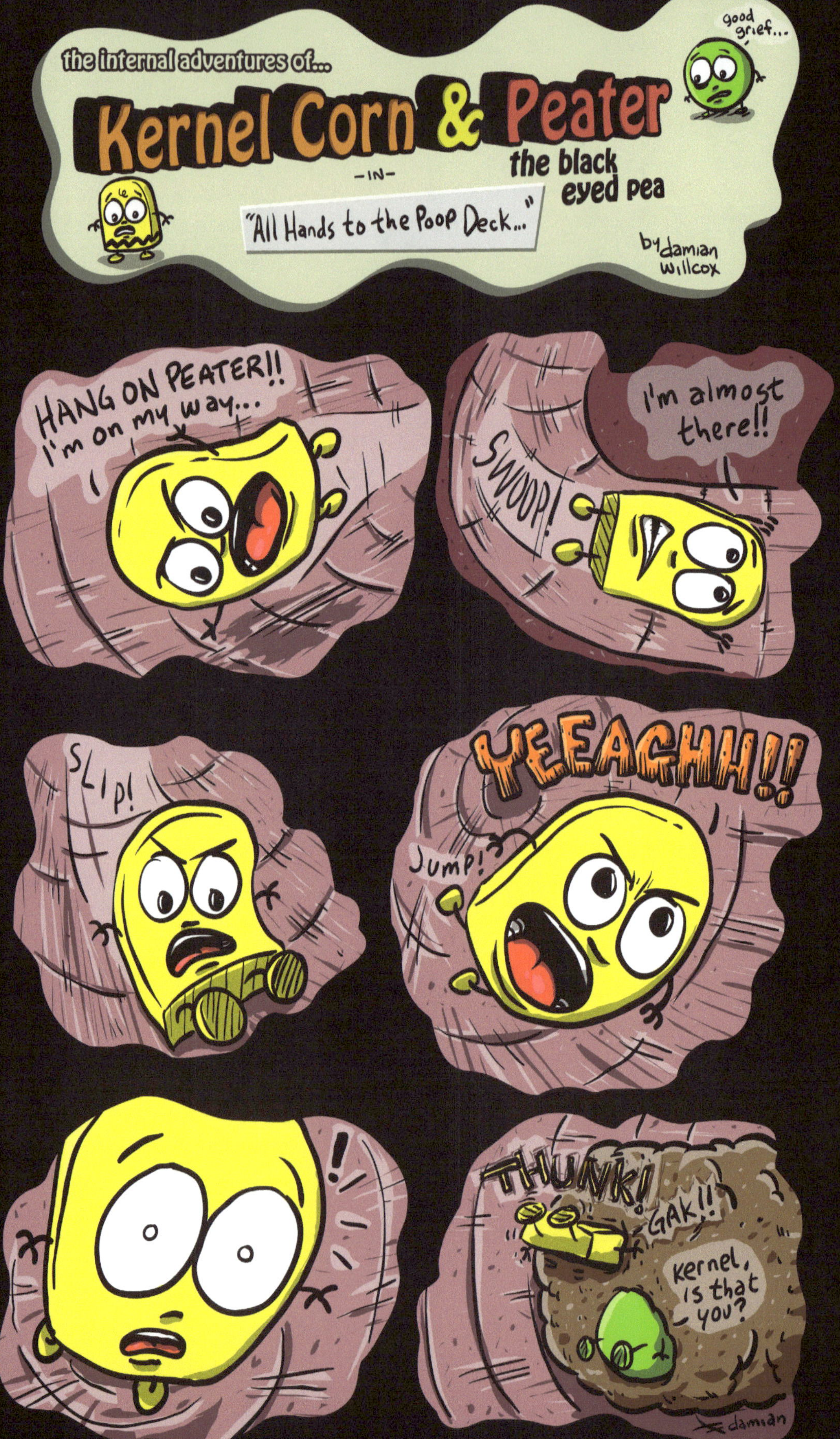

the internal adventures of...
Kernel Corn & Peater
good grief...
-IN-
the black eyed pea
"All Hands to the Poop Deck..."
by damian willcox
HANG ON PEATER!! I'm on my way...
I'm almost there!!
SWOOP!
SLIP!
YEEAGHH!!
JUMP!
!
THUNK!
GAK!!
kernel, is that you?
damian

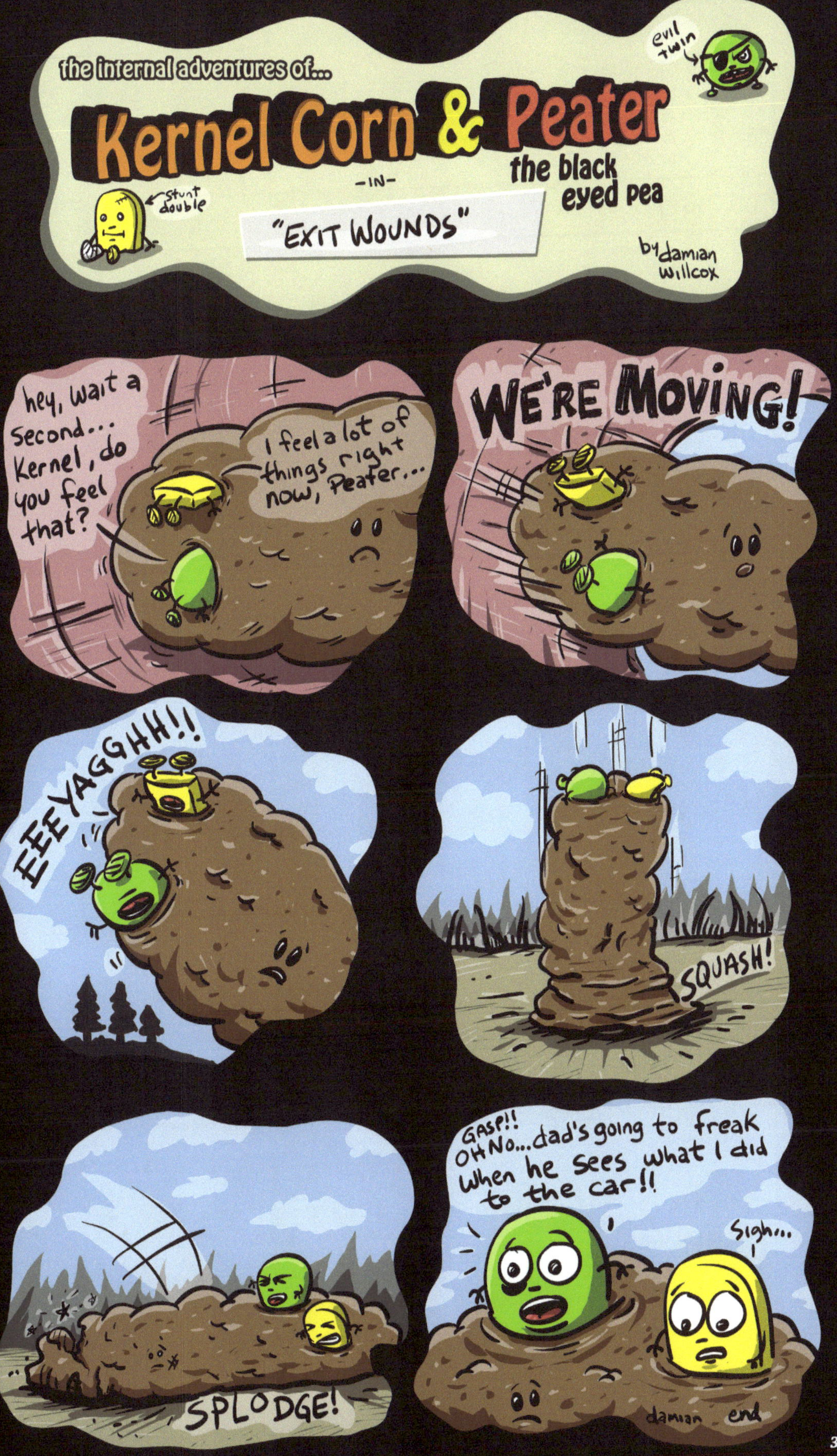

the internal adventures of...
Kernel Corn & Peater
evil twin
-IN-
the black eyed pea
stunt double
"EXIT WOUNDS"
by damian willcox
hey, wait a second... Kernel, do you feel that?
I feel a lot of things right now, Peater...
WE'RE MOVING!
EEEYAGGHH!!
SQUASH!
SPLODGE!
GASP!! OH NO... dad's going to freak when he sees what I did to the car!!
Sigh...
damian
end

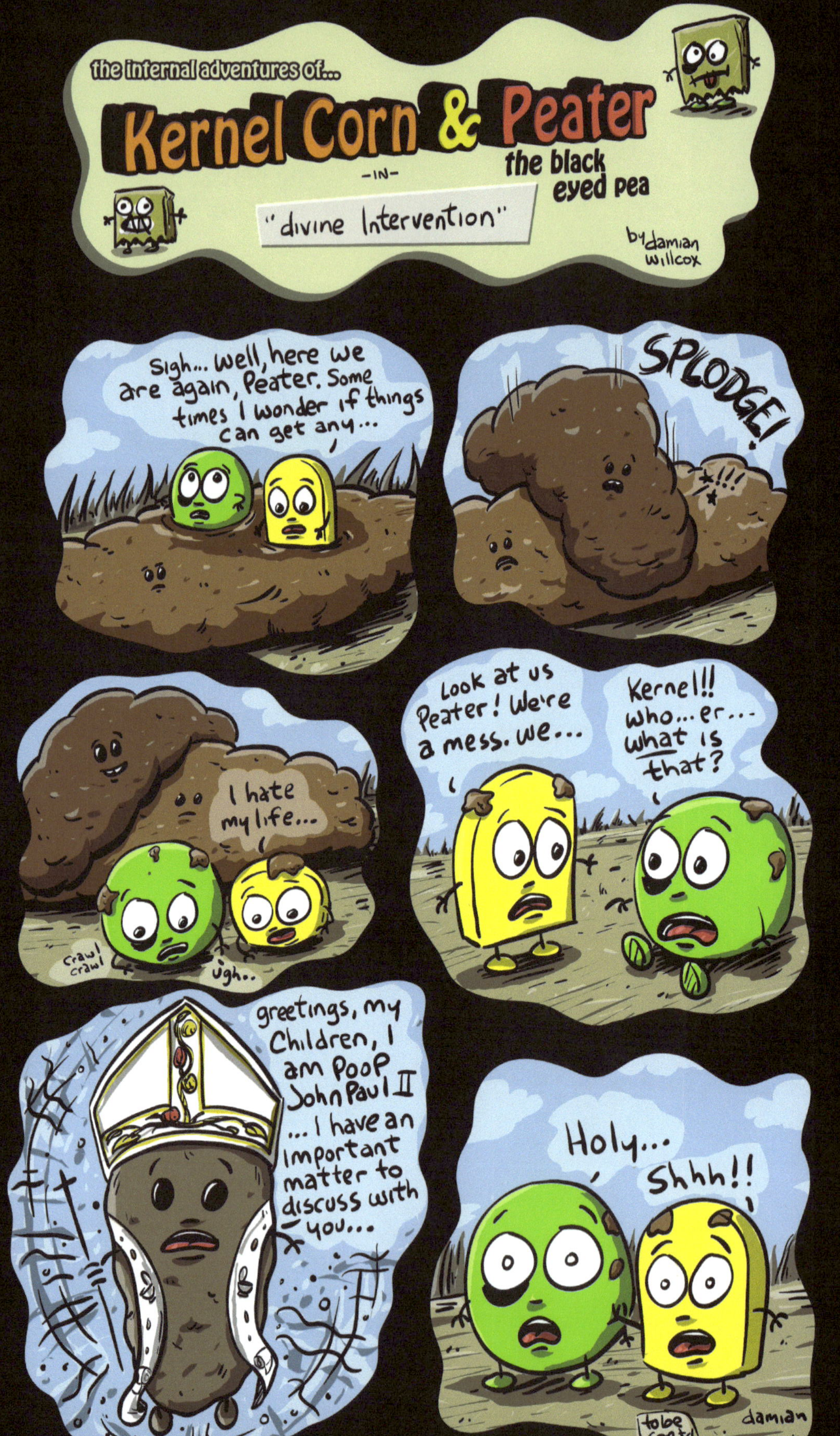

the internal adventures of...
Kernel Corn & Peater
-IN-
the black eyed pea
"divine Intervention"
by damian willcox
Sigh... well, here we are again, Peater. Some times I wonder if things can get any...
SPLODGE!
*!!!
I hate my life...
crawl crawl
ugh..
Look at us Peater! We're a mess. we...
Kernel!! who... er... what is that?
greetings, my Children, I am Poop John Paul II ... I have an important matter to discuss with you...
Holy...
Shhh!!
to be cont'd
damian

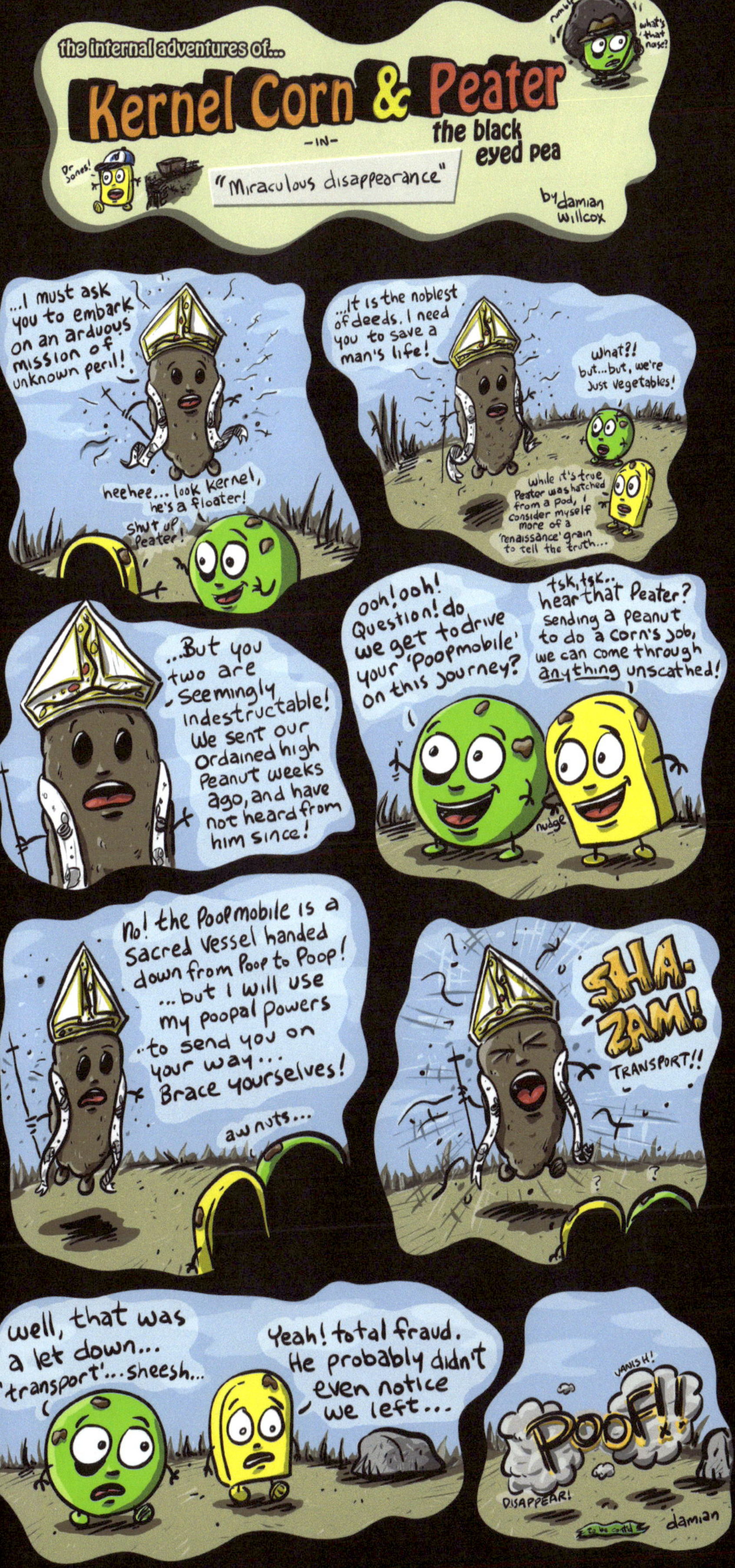
the internal adventures of...
Kernel Corn & Peater
-IN-
the black eyed pea
"Miraculous disappearance"
by damian willcox
Dr Jones!
rumble
what's that noise?
...I must ask you to embark on an arduous mission of unknown peril!
heehee... look kernel, he's a floater!
Shut up Peater!
...It is the noblest of deeds. I need you to save a man's life!
What?! but...but, we're just vegetables!
While it's true Peater was hatched from a pod, I consider myself more of a 'renaissance' grain to tell the truth...
...But you two are seemingly indestructable! We sent our ordained high Peanut weeks ago, and have not heard from him since!
ooh! ooh! Question! do we get to drive your 'poopmobile' on this journey?
tsk, tsk.. hear that Peater? sending a peanut to do a corn's job, we can come through anything unscathed!
nudge
No! the Poopmobile is a Sacred Vessel handed down from Poop to Poop! ...but I will use my poopal powers ..to send you on your way... Brace yourselves!
aw nuts...
SHA-ZAM!
TRANSPORT!!
well, that was a let down... 'transport'... sheesh...
Yeah! total fraud. He probably didn't even notice we left...
VANISH!
POOF!!
DISAPPEAR!
to be cont'd
damian

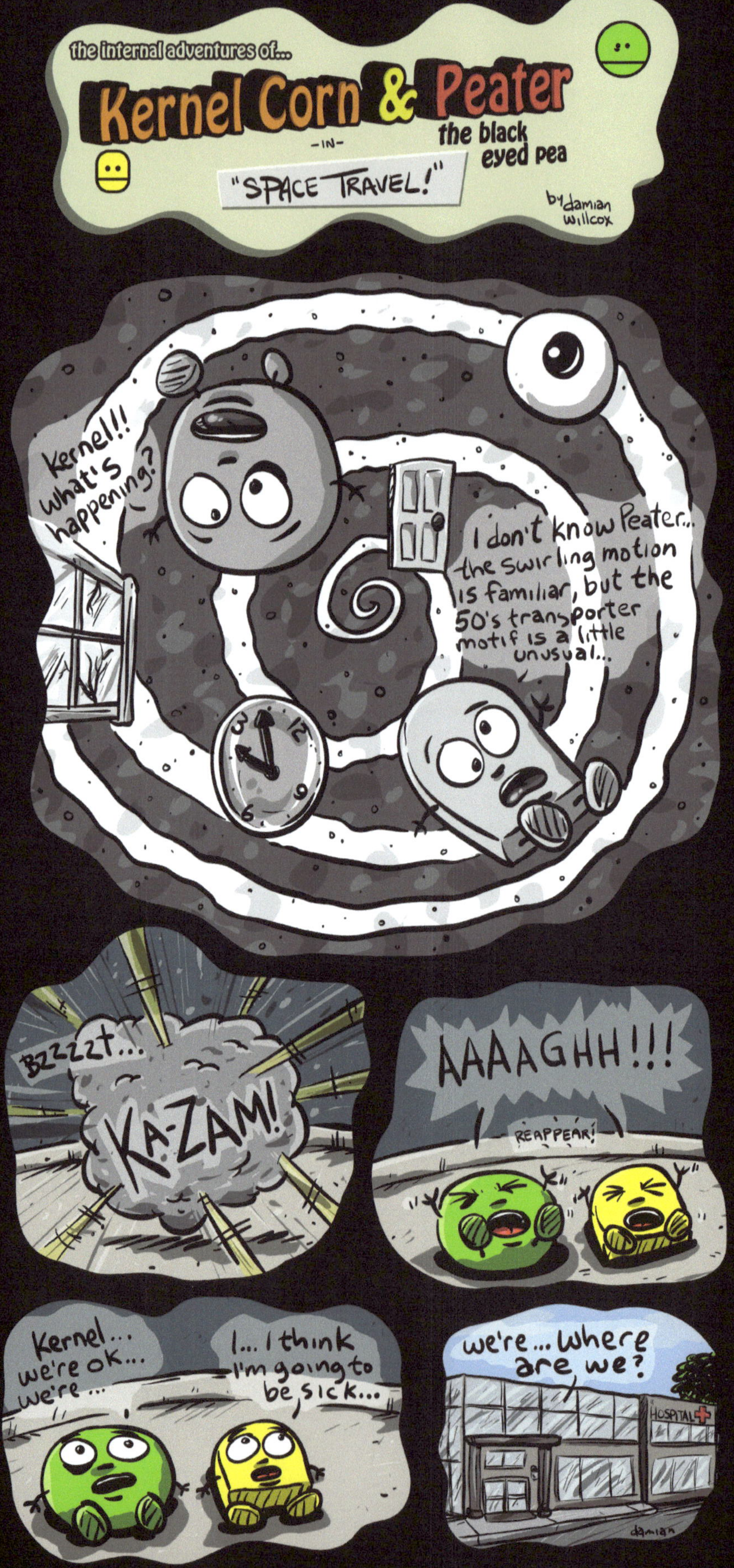
the internal adventures of...
Kernel Corn & Peater the black eyed pea
-IN-
"SPACE TRAVEL!"
by damian willcox
Kernel!! what's happening?
I don't know Peater.. the swirling motion is familiar, but the 50's transporter motif is a little unusual...
Bzzzzt...
KA-ZAM!
AAAAGHH!!!
REAPPEAR!
Kernel... we're ok... we're...
I... I think I'm going to be sick...
we're... where are we?
HOSPITAL
damian

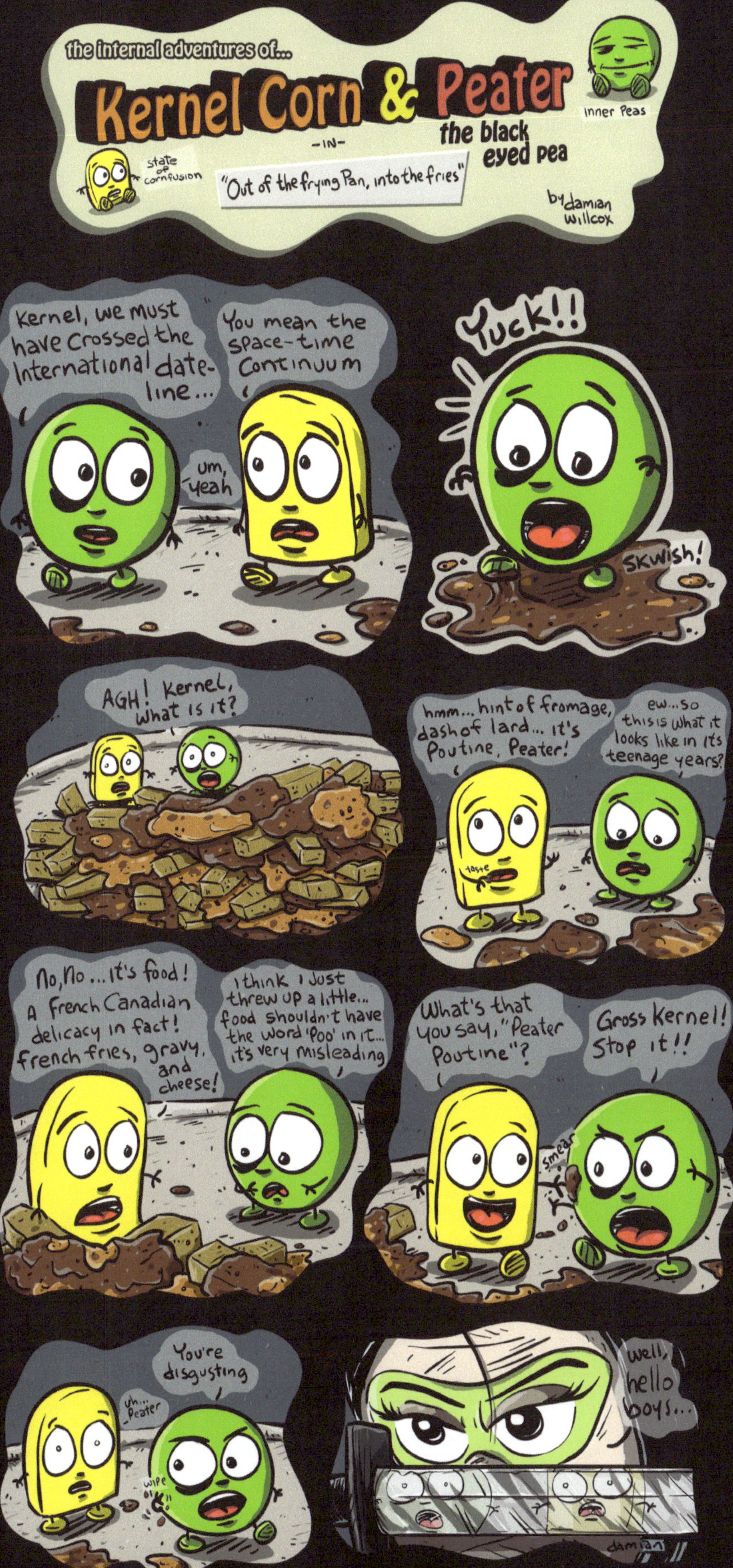
the internal adventures of...
Kernel Corn & Peater
-IN-
the black eyed pea
Inner Peas
State of cornfusion
"Out of the frying Pan, into the fries"
by damian willcox
Kernel, we must have crossed the International date-line...
You mean the space-time continuum
um, yeah
Yuck!!
SKWISH!
AGH! Kernel, what is it?
hmm... hint of fromage, dash of lard... it's Poutine, Peater!
taste
ew...so this is what it looks like in its teenage years?
No, No ... it's food! A French Canadian delicacy in fact! French fries, gravy, and cheese!
I think I just threw up a little... food shouldn't have the word 'Poo' in it... it's very misleading
What's that you say, "Peater Poutine"?
smear
Gross Kernel! Stop it!!
You're disgusting
uh... Peater
wipe
well, hello boys...
damian

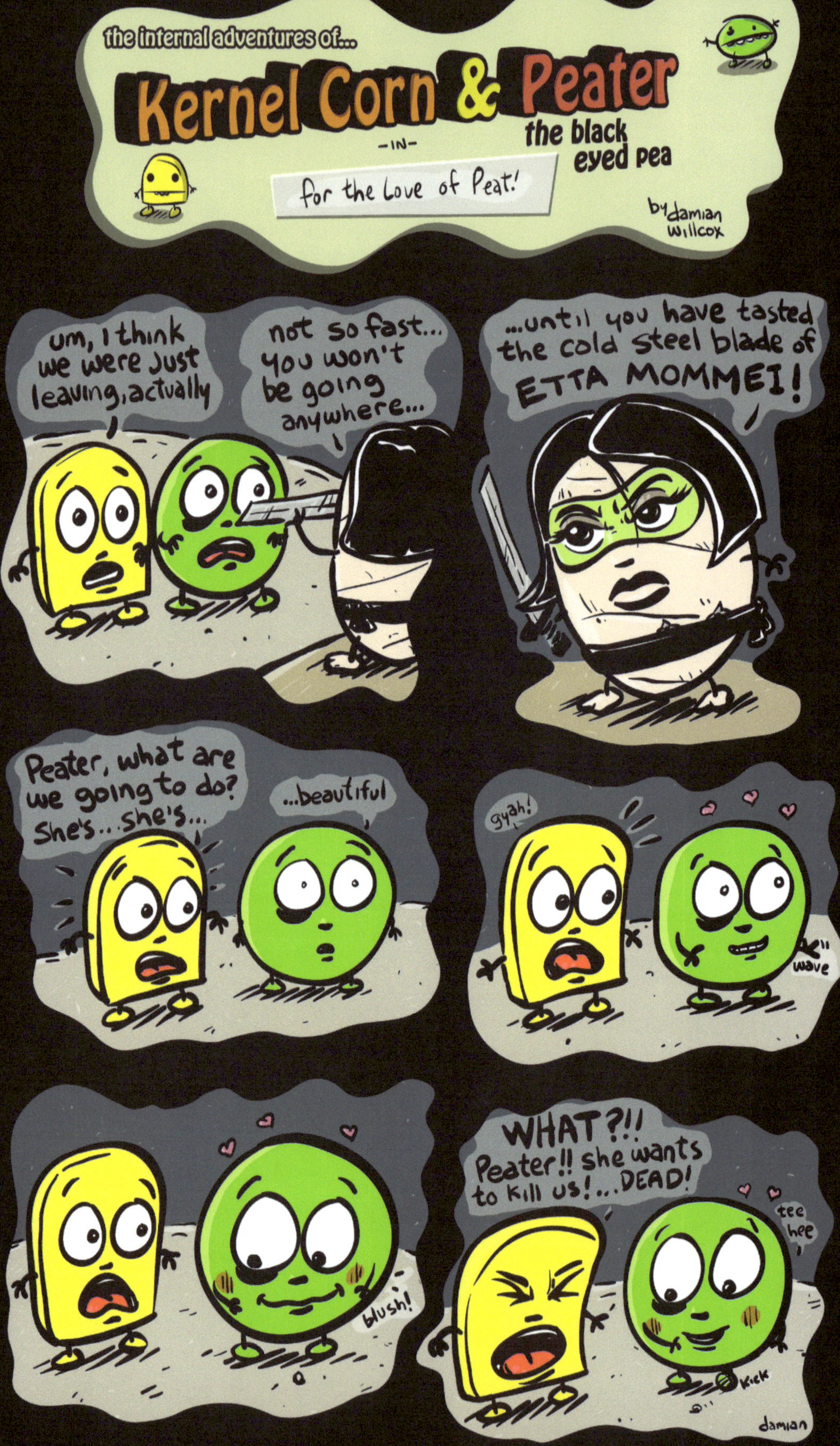
the internal adventures of...
Kernel Corn & Peater
-IN-
the black eyed pea
for the Love of Peat!
by damian willcox
um, I think we were just leaving, actually
not so fast... you won't be going anywhere...
...until you have tasted the cold steel blade of ETTA MOMMEI!
Peater, what are we going to do? She's... she's...
...beautiful
gyah!
wave
blush!
WHAT?!! Peater!! she wants to kill us!... DEAD!
tee hee
kick
damian

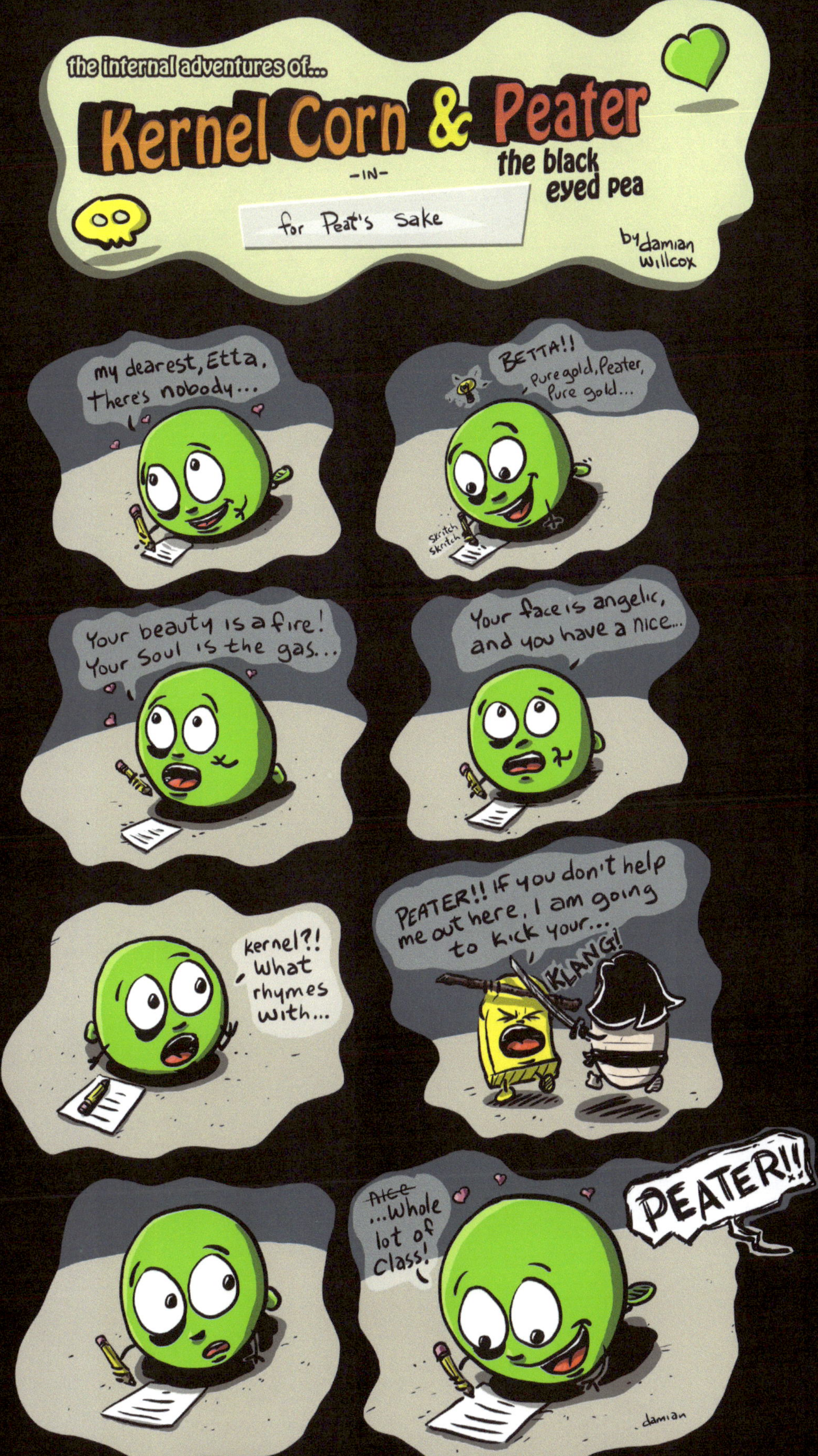
the internal adventures of...
Kernel Corn & Peater
-IN-
the black eyed pea
for Peat's sake
by damian willcox
my dearest, Etta, there's nobody...
BETTA!!
Pure gold, Peater, Pure gold...
Skritch Skritch
Your beauty is a fire! Your Soul is the gas...
Your face is angelic, and you have a nice...
kernel?! What rhymes with...
PEATER!! If you don't help me out here, I am going to kick your...
KLANG!
~~nice~~ ...whole lot of class!
PEATER!!
damian

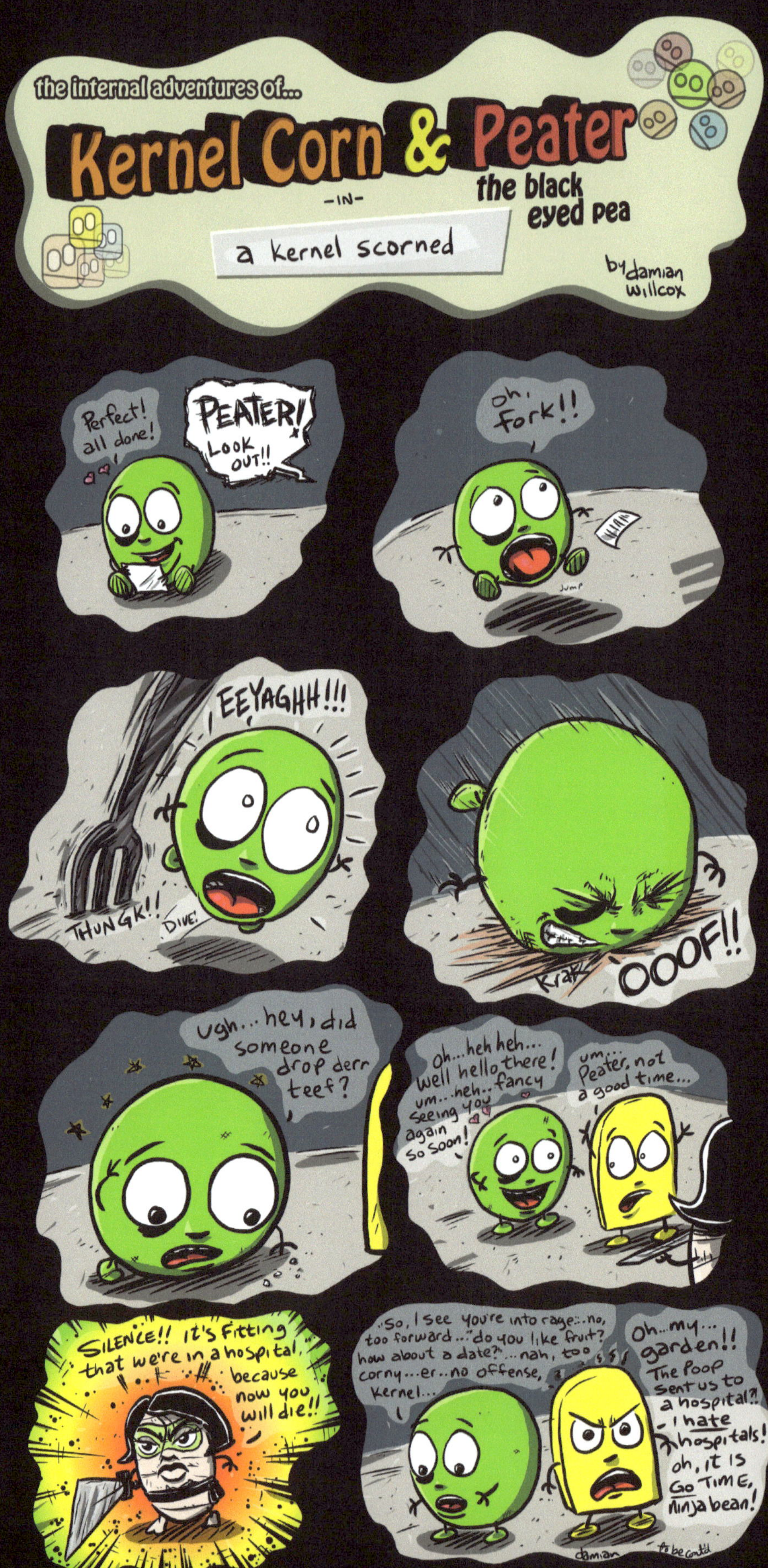
the internal adventures of...
Kernel Corn & Peater the black eyed pea
-IN-
a kernel scorned
by damian willcox
Perfect! all done!
PEATER! LOOK OUT!!
oh, fork!!
JUMP
EEYAGHH!!!
THUNGK!!
DIVE!
KRAK
OOOF!!
ugh... hey, did someone drop derr teef?
oh...heh heh... well hello there! um...heh.. fancy seeing you again so soon!
um... Peater, not a good time...
SILENCE!! It's fitting that we're in a hospital, because now you will die!!
"So, I see you're into rage::.no, too forward..."do you like fruit?" how about a date?"...nah, too corny...er..no offense, Kernel...
Oh...my... garden!! The Poop sent us to a hospital?! I hate hospitals! oh, it is GO TIME, ninja bean!
damian
to be cont'd

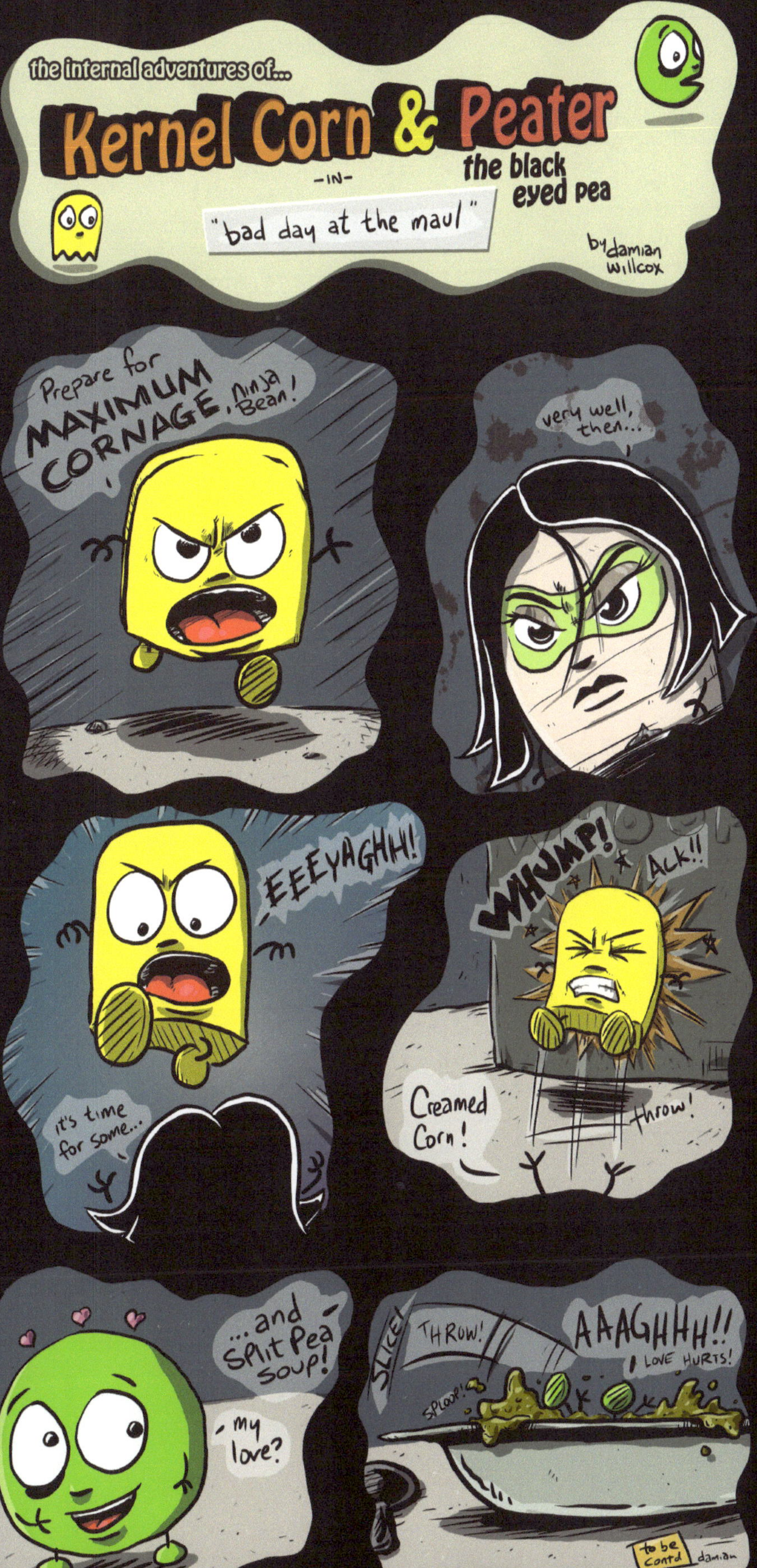
the internal adventures of...
Kernel Corn & Peater
-IN-
the black eyed pea
"bad day at the maul"
by damian willcox
Prepare for MAXIMUM CORNAGE, Ninja Bean!
very well, then...
EEEYAGHH!
it's time for some...
WHUMP!
ACK!!
Creamed Corn!
throw!
...and Split Pea Soup!
my love?
SLICE!
THROW!
SPLOOP!
AAAGHHH!!
LOVE HURTS!
to be contd
damian

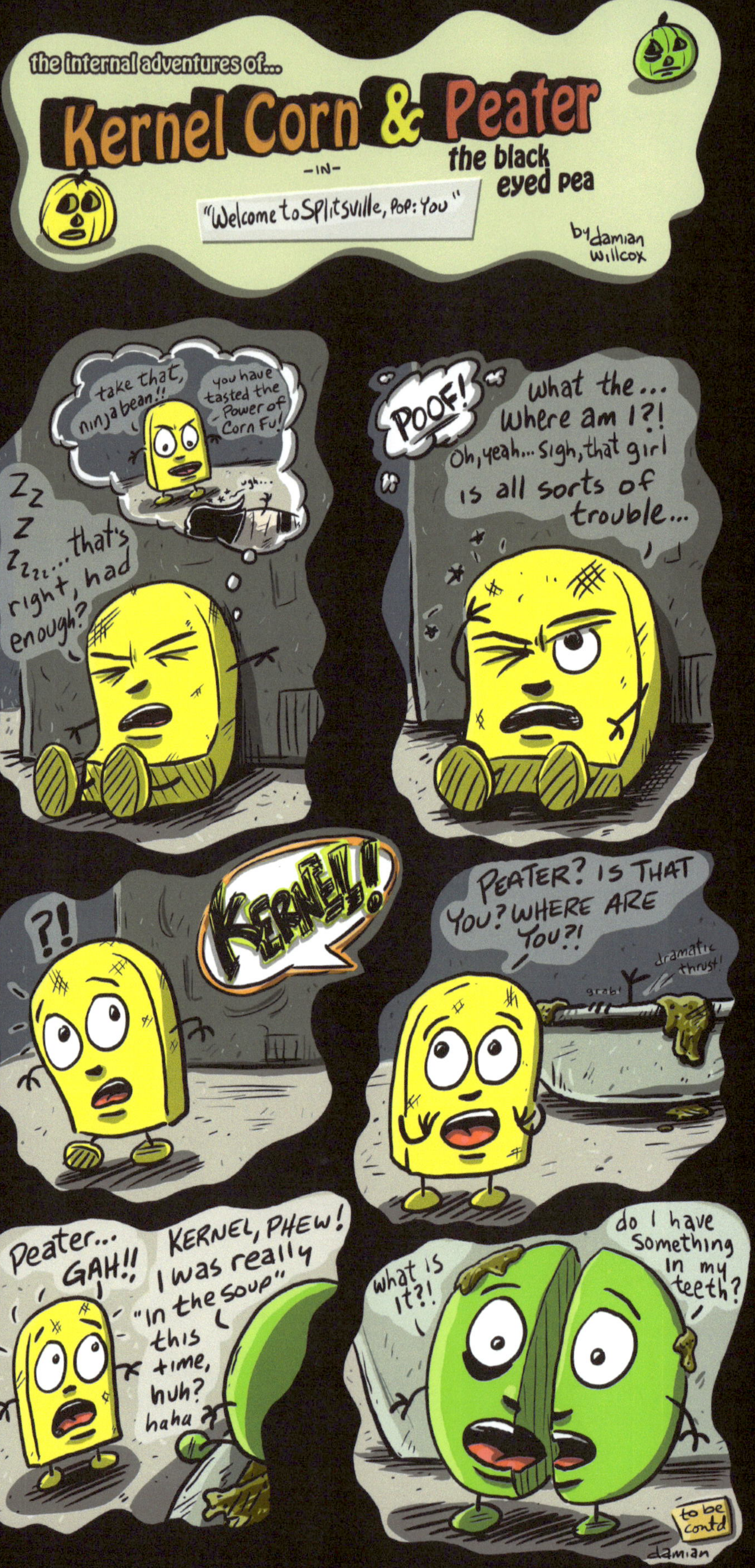

the internal adventures of...
Kernel Corn & Peater
-IN-
the black eyed pea
"Welcome to Splitsville, Pop: You"
by damian willcox
take that, ninja bean!!
you have tasted the Power of Corn Fu!
ugh...
Z Z Z Zzz... that's right, had enough?
POOF!
what the... where am I?! Oh, yeah... sigh, that girl is all sorts of trouble...
?!
KERNEL!!
PEATER? IS THAT YOU? WHERE ARE YOU?!
grab!
dramatic thrust!
Peater... GAH!!
KERNEL, PHEW! I was really "in the soup" this time, huh? haha
what is it?!
do I have something in my teeth?
to be cont'd
damian

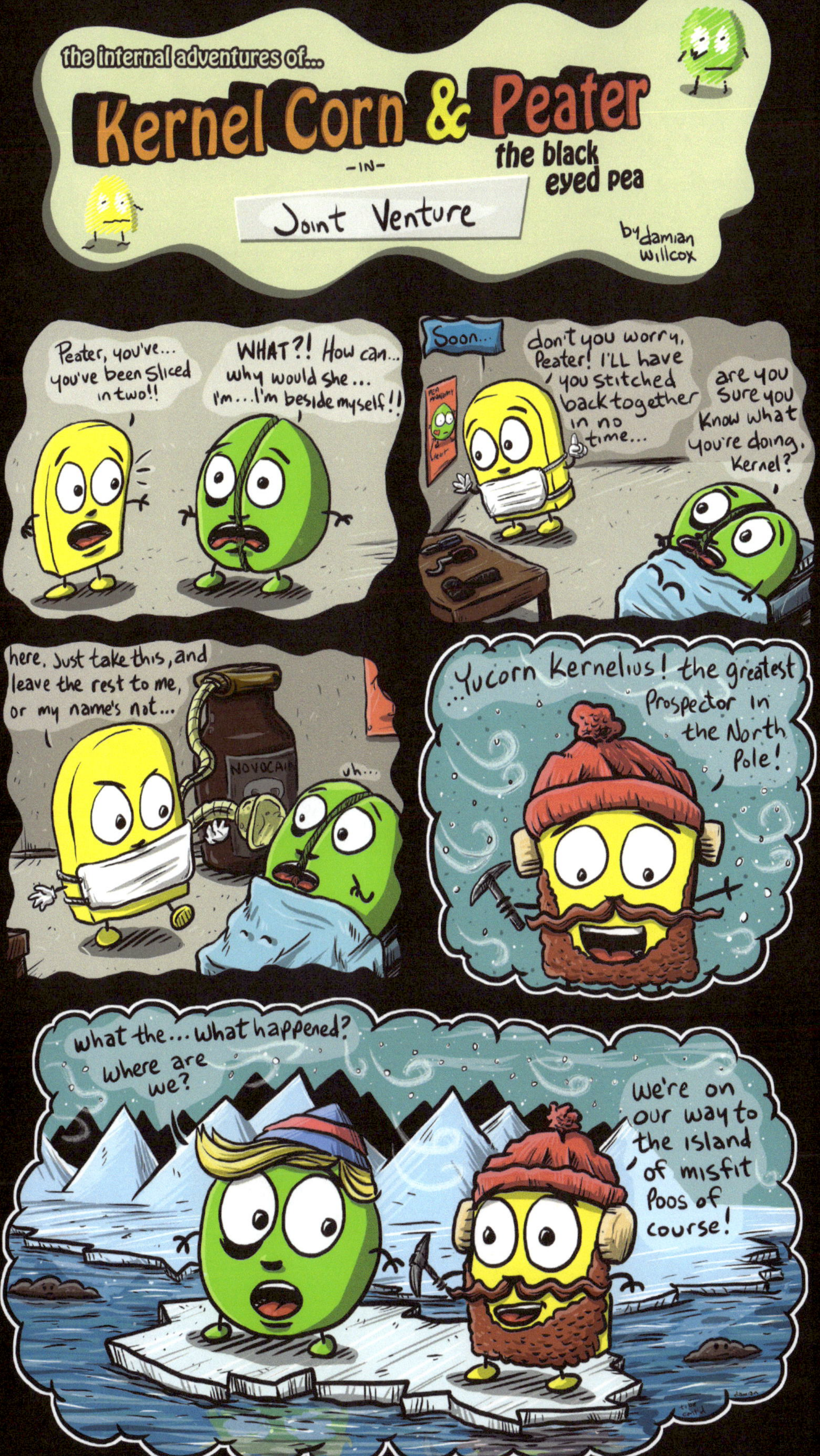
the internal adventures of...
Kernel Corn & Peater
the black eyed pea
-IN-
Joint Venture
by damian willcox
Peater, you've... you've been sliced in two!!
WHAT?! How can... why would she... I'm...I'm beside myself!!
Soon...
don't you worry, Peater! I'LL have you stitched back together in no time...
are you sure you know what you're doing, Kernel?
here. Just take this, and leave the rest to me, or my name's not...
NOVOCAIN
uh...
...Yucorn Kernelius! the greatest Prospector in the North Pole!
what the... what happened? where are we?
We're on our way to the island of misfit Poos of course!

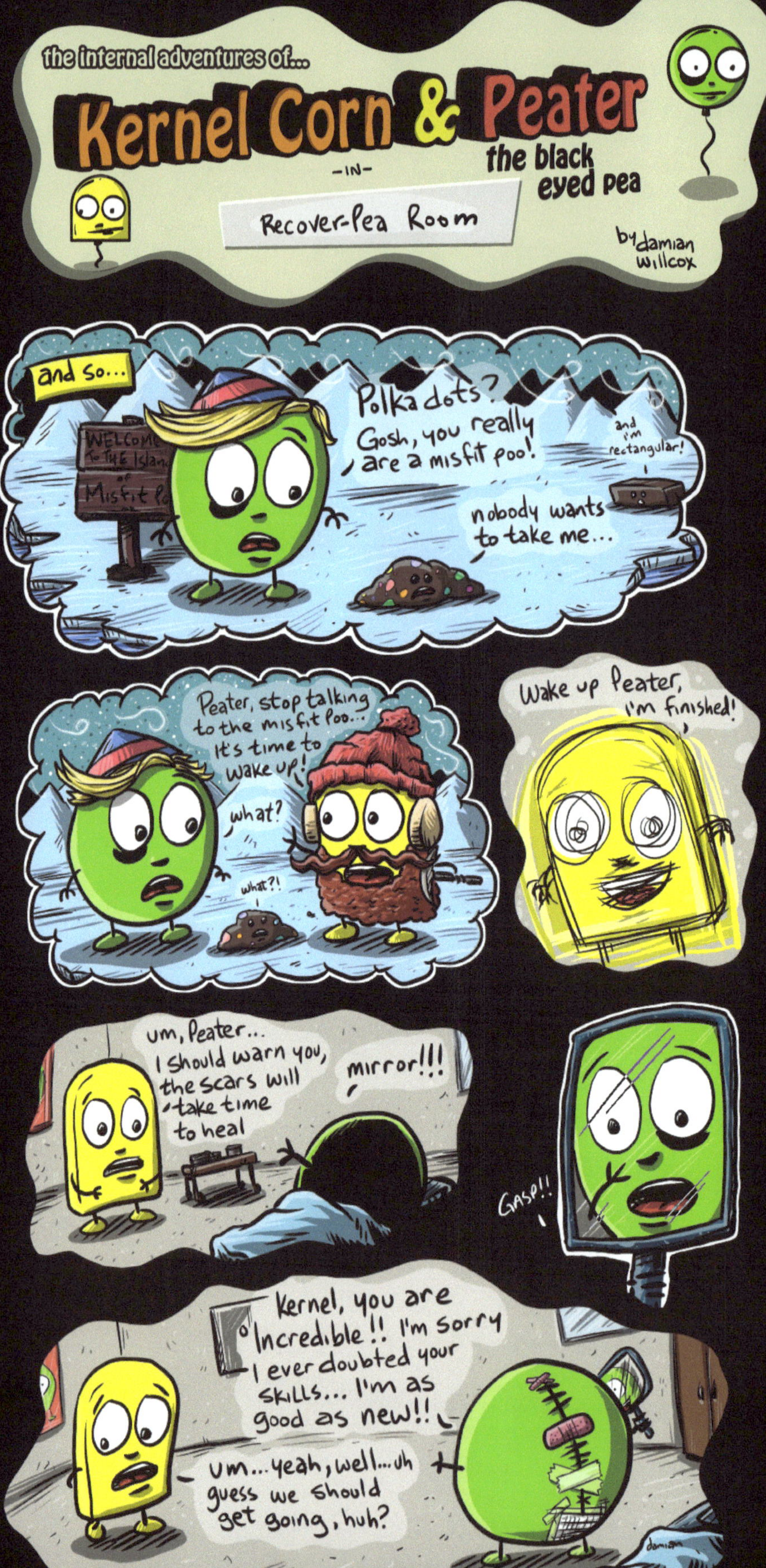

the internal adventures of...
Kernel Corn & Peater
-IN-
the black eyed pea
Recover-Pea Room
by damian willcox
and so...
WELCOME TO THE Island of Misfit P
Polka dots? Gosh, you really are a misfit poo!
and i'm rectangular!
nobody wants to take me...
Peater, stop talking to the misfit Poo... It's time to wake up!
what?
what?!
Wake up Peater, I'm finished!
um, Peater... I should warn you, the scars will take time to heal
mirror!!!
GASP!!
Kernel, you are Incredible!! I'm sorry I ever doubted your skills... I'm as good as new!!
um...yeah, well...uh guess we should get going, huh?
damian

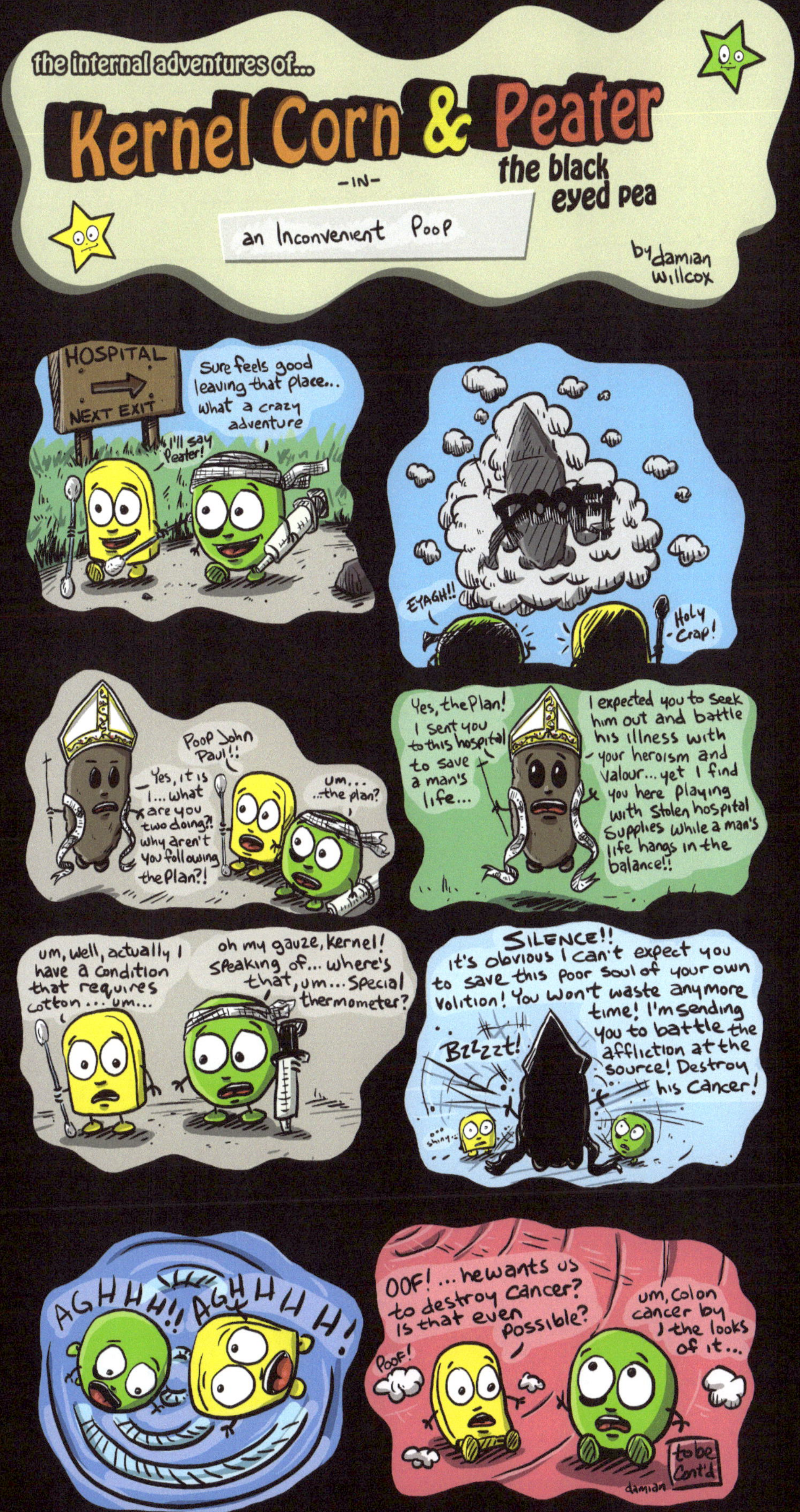
the internal adventures of...
Kernel Corn & Peater the black eyed pea
-IN-
an Inconvenient Poop
by damian willcox
HOSPITAL NEXT EXIT
Sure feels good leaving that place... what a crazy adventure
I'll say Peater!
POOP!
EYAGH!!
Holy Crap!
Poop John Paul!!
Yes, it is I... what are you two doing?! why aren't you following the Plan?!
um... ...the plan?
Yes, the Plan! I sent you to this hospital to save a man's life...
I expected you to seek him out and battle his illness with your heroism and valour... yet I find you here playing with stolen hospital supplies while a man's life hangs in the balance!!
um, well, actually I have a condition that requires cotton... um...
oh my gauze, Kernel! Speaking of... where's that, um... special thermometer?
SILENCE!! It's obvious I can't expect you to save this poor soul of your own volition! You won't waste anymore time! I'm sending you to battle the affliction at the source! Destroy his cancer!
Bzzzzt!
AGHHH!! AGHHHHH!
OOF! ... he wants us to destroy cancer? Is that even possible?
POOF!
um, colon cancer by the looks of it...
to be Cont'd
damian

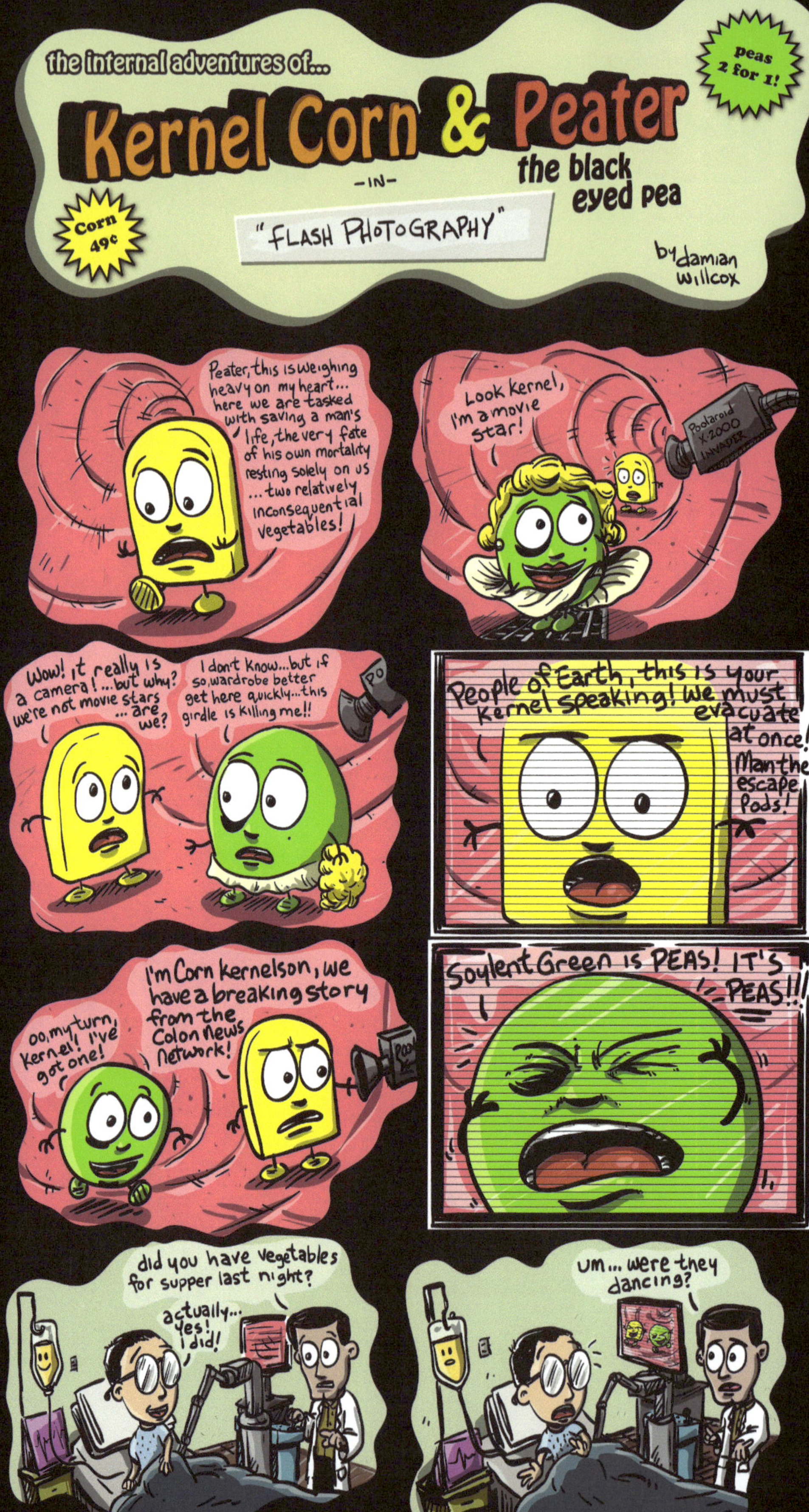

the internal adventures of...
Kernel Corn & Peater
-IN-
the black eyed pea
peas 2 for 1!
Corn 49¢
"FLASH PHOTOGRAPHY"
by damian willcox
Peater, this is weighing heavy on my heart... here we are tasked with saving a man's life, the very fate of his own mortality resting solely on us ...two relatively inconsequential vegetables!
Look kernel, I'm a movie star!
Pooloroid X-2000 INVADER
Wow! it really is a camera! ...but why? we're not movie stars ...are we?
I don't know...but if so, wardrobe better get here quickly...this girdle is killing me!!
People of Earth, this is your kernel speaking! We must evacuate at once! Man the escape pods!
oo, my turn, kernel! I've got one!
I'm Corn kernelson, we have a breaking story from the Colon News Network!
Soylent Green is PEAS! IT'S PEAS!!!
did you have vegetables for supper last night?
actually... yes! I did!
um... were they dancing?

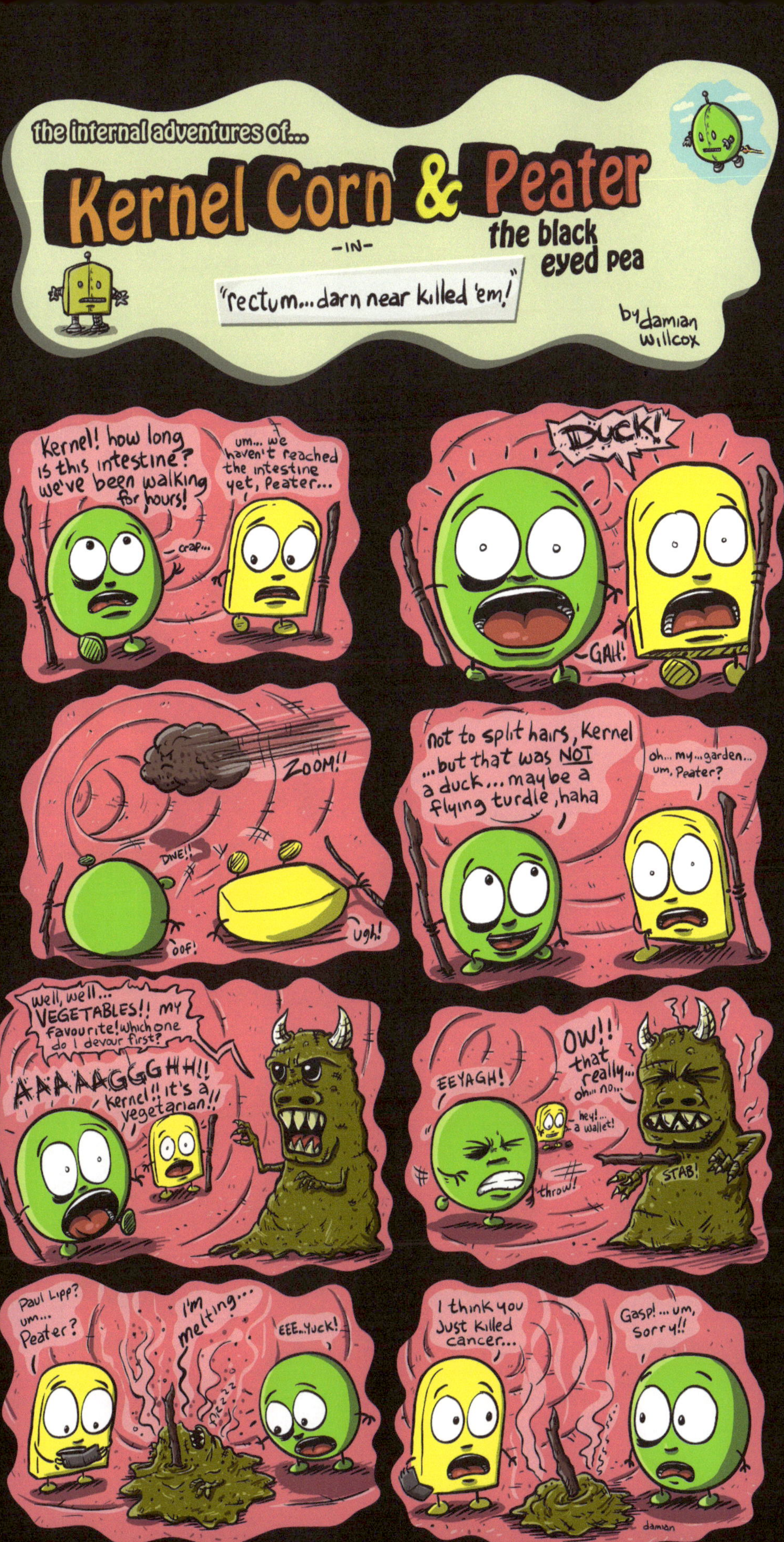

the internal adventures of...
Kernel Corn & Peater
-IN-
the black eyed pea
"rectum...darn near killed 'em!"
by damian willcox
Kernel! how long is this intestine? we've been walking for hours!
um... we haven't reached the intestine yet, Peater...
-crap...
DUCK!
GAH!
ZOOM!!
OWE!!
OOF!
ugh!
not to split hairs, Kernel ...but that was NOT a duck... maybe a flying turdle, haha
oh... my...garden... um, Peater?
well, well... VEGETABLES!! my favourite! which one do I devour first?
AAAAAGGGHH!! Kernel!! it's a vegetarian!!
EEYAGH!
OW!! that really... oh... no...
hey!... a wallet!
throw!
STAB!
Paul Lipp? um... Peater?
I'm melting...
EEE..YUCK!
I think you just killed cancer...
Gasp!... um, sorry!!
damian

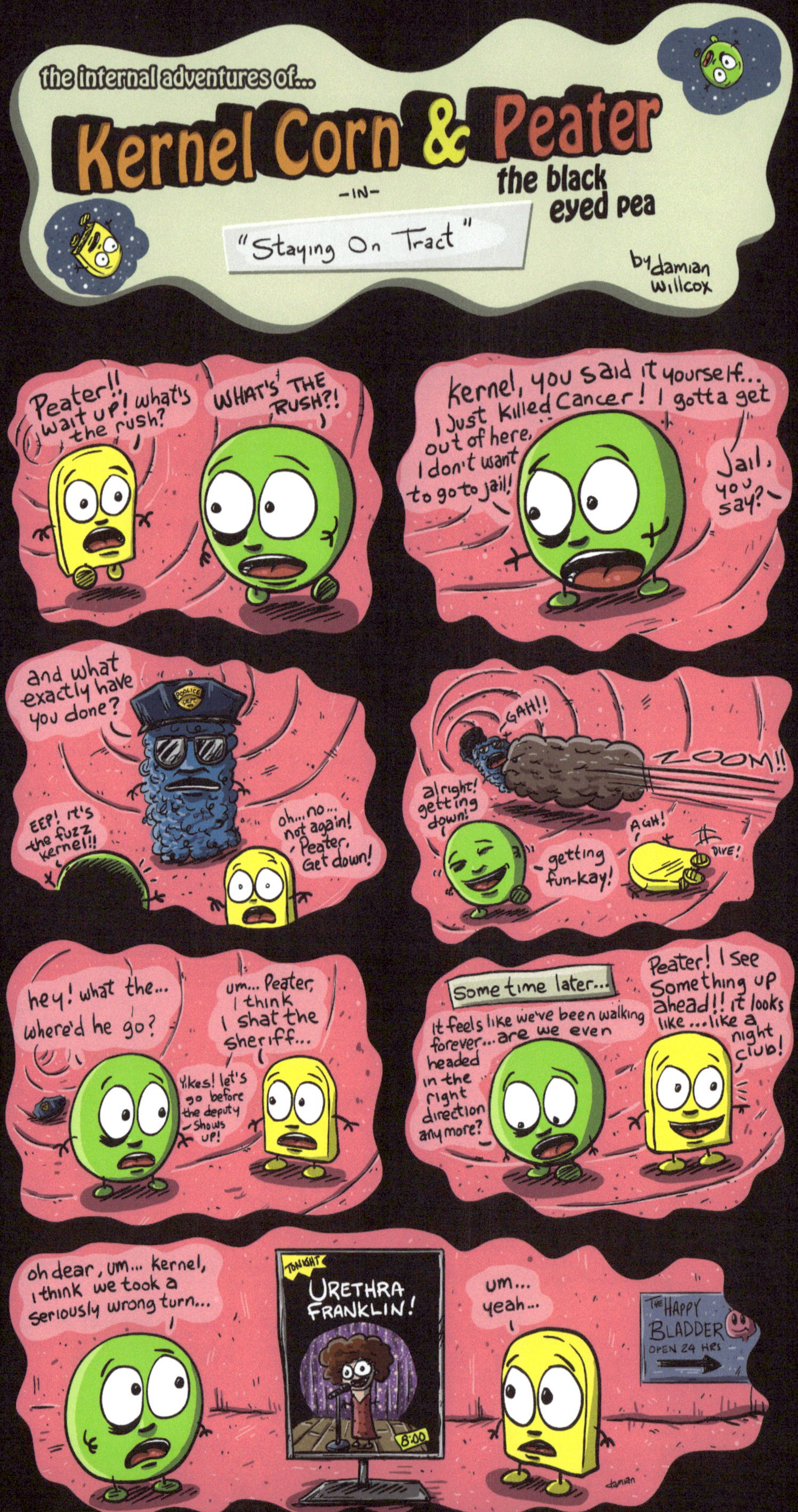

the internal adventures of...
Kernel Corn & Peater the black eyed pea
-IN-
"Staying On Tract"
by damian willcox
Peater!! wait up! what's the rush?
WHAT'S THE RUSH?!
Kernel, you said it yourself... I just killed Cancer! I gotta get out of here, I don't want to go to jail!
Jail, you say?
and what exactly have you done?
POLICE DEPT
EEP! it's the fuzz kernel!!
oh...no... not again! Peater, Get down!
GAH!!
ZOOM!!
alright! getting down!
getting fun-kay!
AGH!
DIVE!
hey! what the... where'd he go?
um... Peater, I think I shat the sheriff...
Yikes! let's go before the deputy shows up!
Some time later...
It feels like we've been walking forever... are we even headed in the right direction any more?
Peater! I see something up ahead!! it looks like...like a night club!
oh dear, um... kernel, I think we took a seriously wrong turn...
TONIGHT
URETHRA FRANKLIN!
8:00
um... yeah...
THE HAPPY BLADDER
OPEN 24 HRS
damian

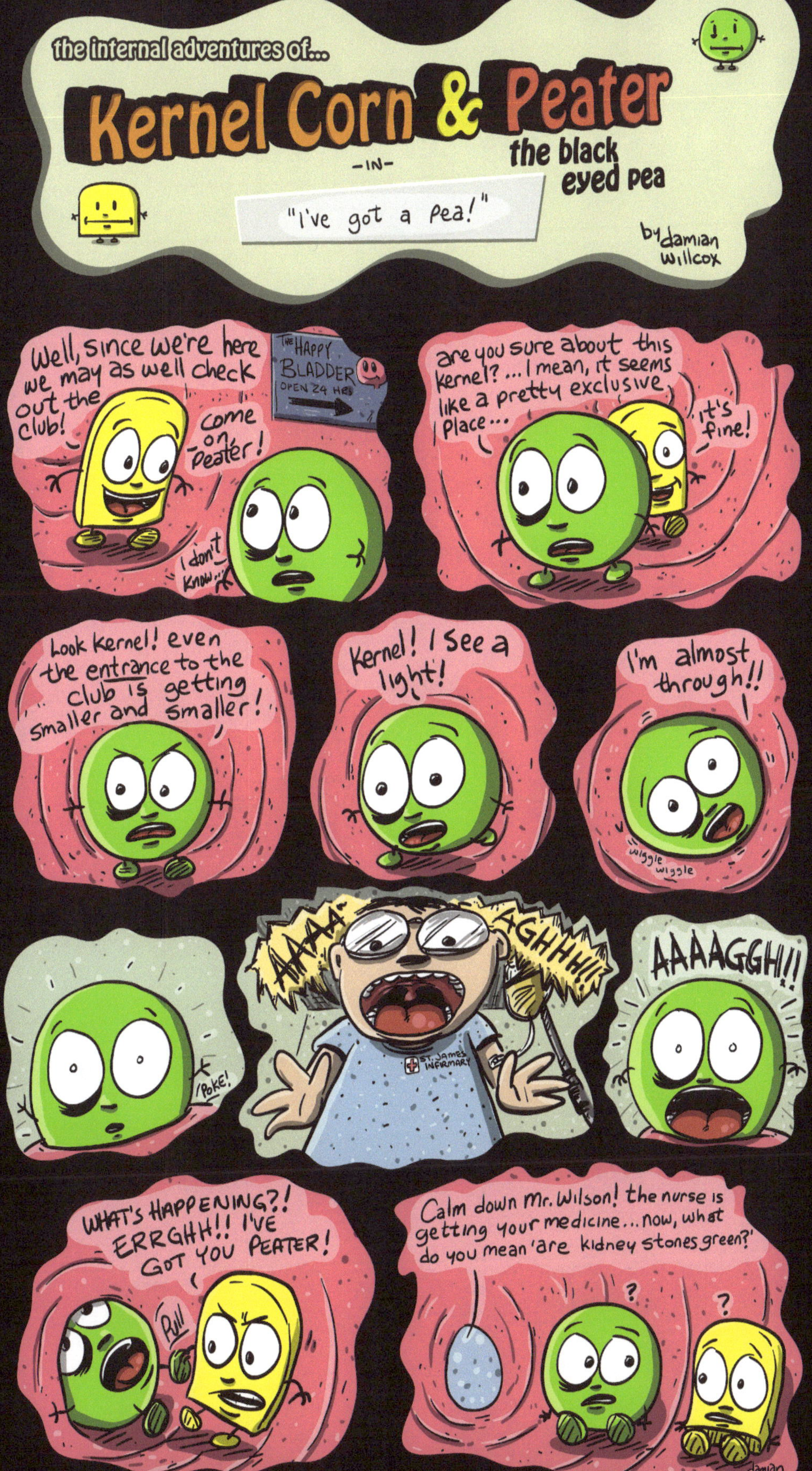
the internal adventures of...
Kernel Corn & Peater
-IN-
the black eyed pea
"I've got a pea!"
by damian willcox
Well, since we're here we may as well check out the club!
THE HAPPY BLADDER OPEN 24 HRS
come on Peater!
I don't know...
are you sure about this kernel? ... I mean, it seems like a pretty exclusive place...
it's fine!
Look kernel! even the entrance to the club is getting smaller and smaller!
Kernel! I see a light!
I'm almost through!!
wiggle wiggle
POKE!
AAAAAGHHH!!
ST. JAMES INFIRMARY
AAAAGGH!!
WHAT'S HAPPENING?! ERRGHH!! I'VE GOT YOU PEATER!
PULL
Calm down Mr. Wilson! the nurse is getting your medicine... now, what do you mean 'are kidney stones green?'
?
?
damian

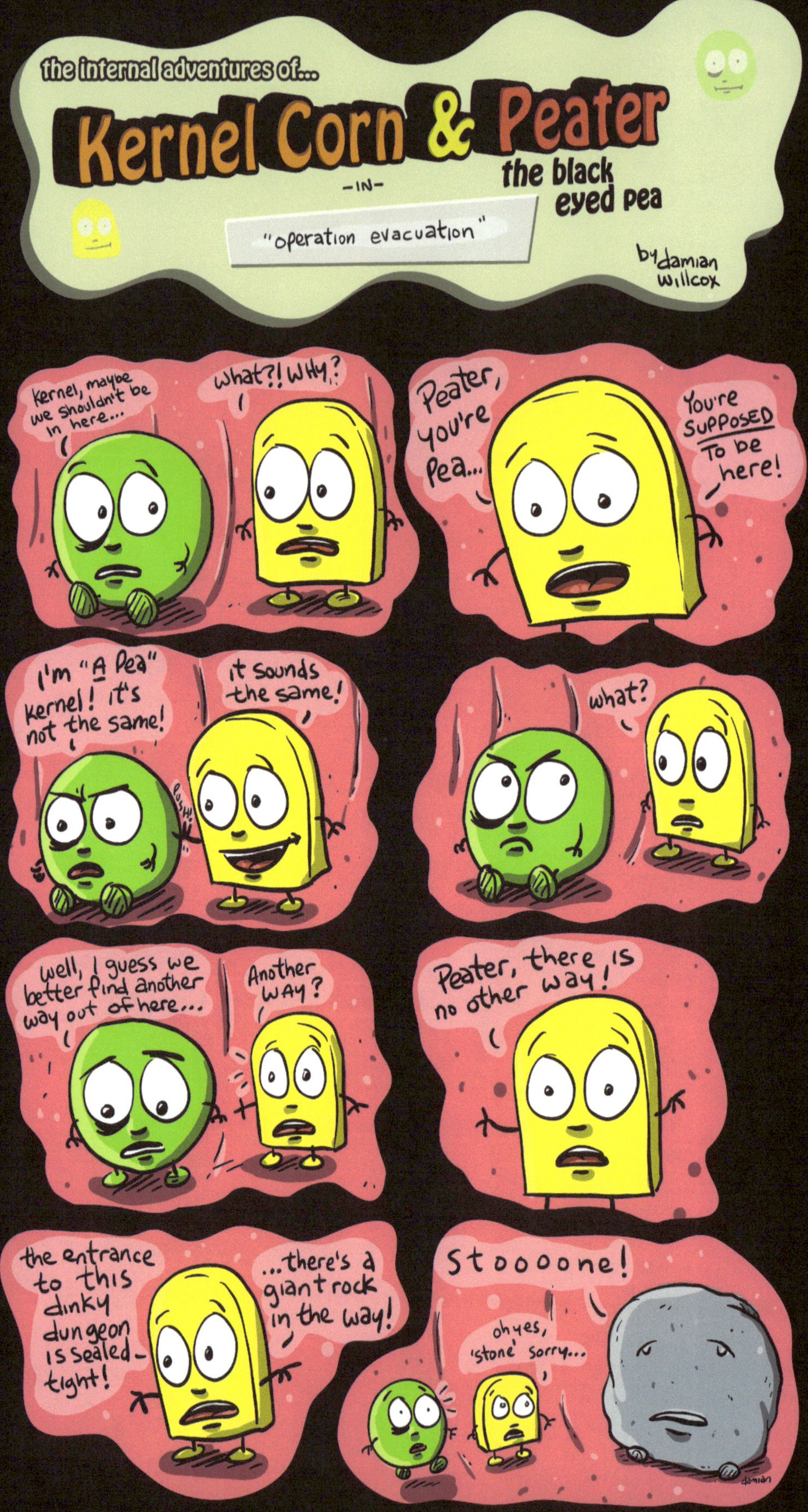

the internal adventures of...
Kernel Corn & Peater
-IN-
the black eyed pea
"operation evacuation"
by damian willcox
Kernel, maybe we shouldn't be in here...
what?! WHY?
Peater, you're Pea...
You're SUPPOSED To be here!
I'm "A Pea" kernel! it's not the same!
it sounds the same!
what?
well, I guess we better find another way out of here...
Another WAY?
Peater, there is no other way!
the entrance to this dinky dungeon is sealed-tight!
...there's a giant rock in the way!
Stoooone!
oh yes, 'stone' sorry...

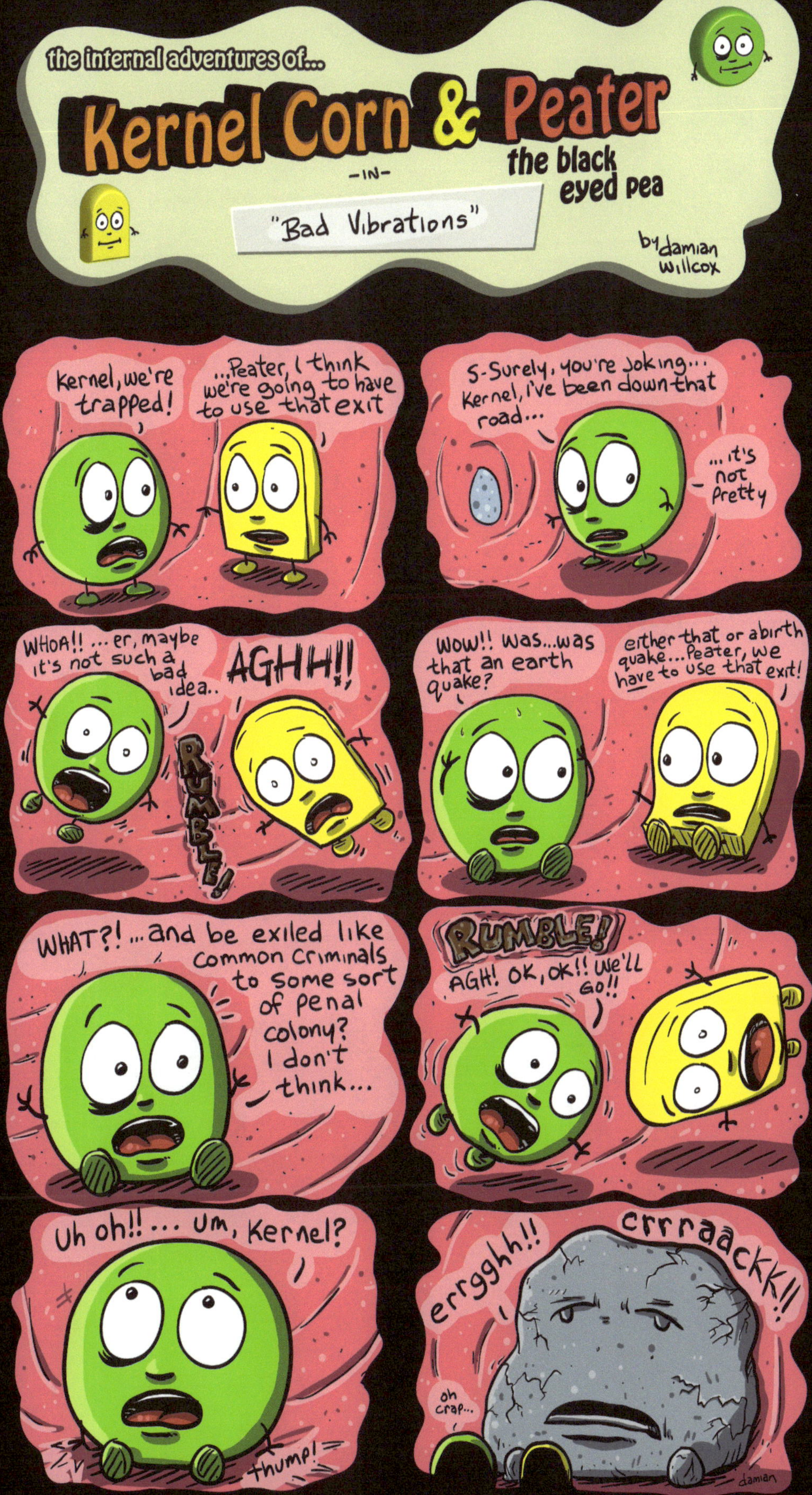
the internal adventures of...
Kernel Corn & Peater the black eyed pea
-IN-
"Bad Vibrations"
by damian willcox
Kernel, we're trapped!
...Peater, I think we're going to have to use that exit
S-Surely, you're joking... Kernel, I've been down that road...
...it's not pretty
WHOA!! ...er, maybe it's not such a bad idea..
AGHH!!
RUMBLE!
WOW!! Was...was that an earth quake?
either that or a birth quake...Peater, we have to use that exit!
WHAT?! ...and be exiled like common criminals to some sort of penal colony? I don't think...
RUMBLE!
AGH! OK, OK!! We'll GO!!
Uh oh!! ... Um, Kernel?
thump!
errgghh!!
crrraackk!!
oh crap...
damian

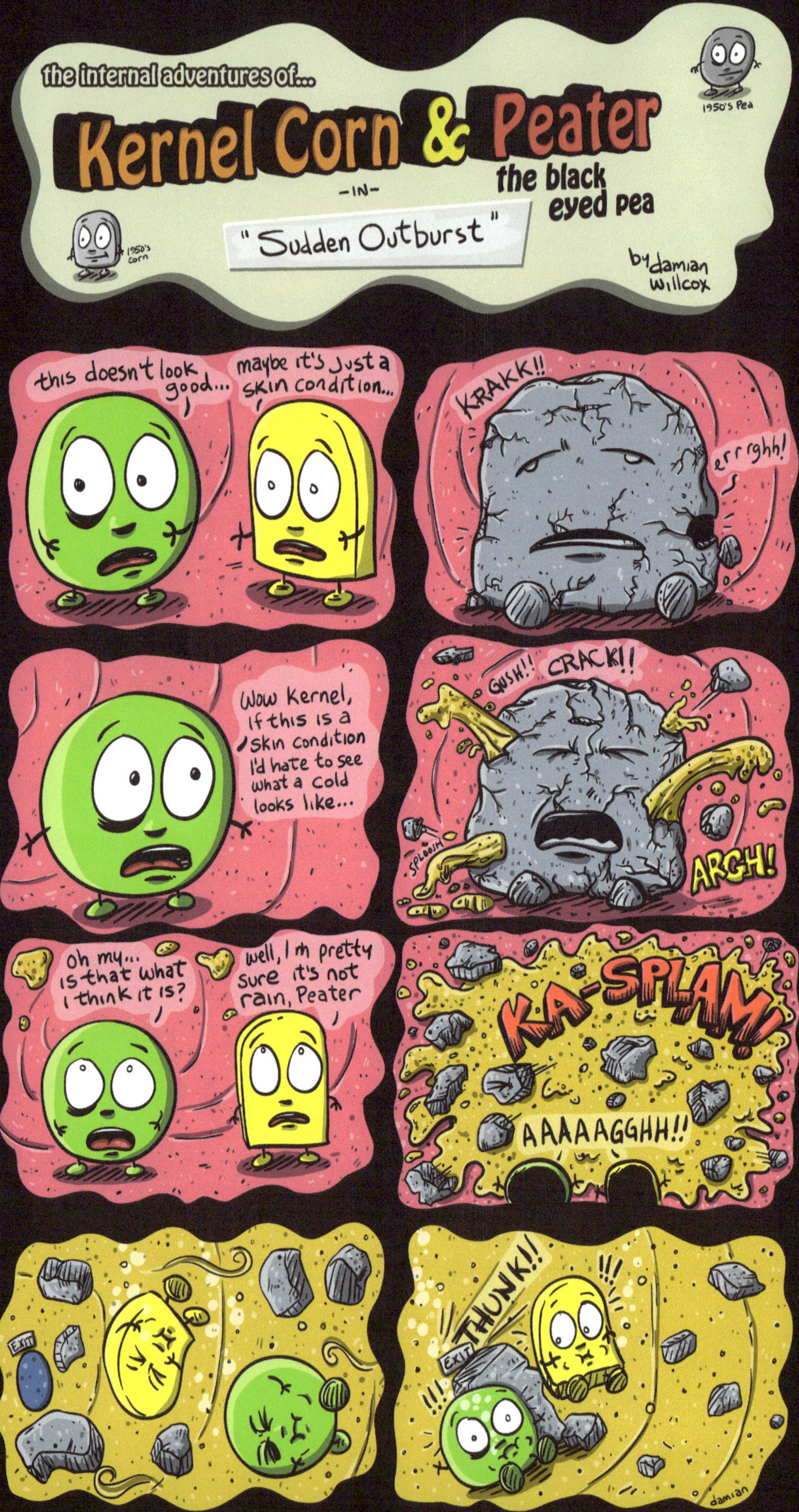
the internal adventures of...
Kernel Corn & Peater
1950's Pea
-IN-
the black eyed pea
1950's corn
"Sudden Outburst"
by damian willcox
this doesn't look good...
maybe it's just a skin condition...
KRAKK!!
errrghh!
Wow Kernel, If this is a skin condition I'd hate to see what a cold looks like...
GUSH!!
CRACK!!
SPLOOSH
ARGH!
oh my... is that what i think it is?
well, I'm pretty sure it's not rain, Peater
KA-SPLAM!
AAAAAGGHH!!
EXIT
THUNK!!
!!!
EXIT
!!!
damian

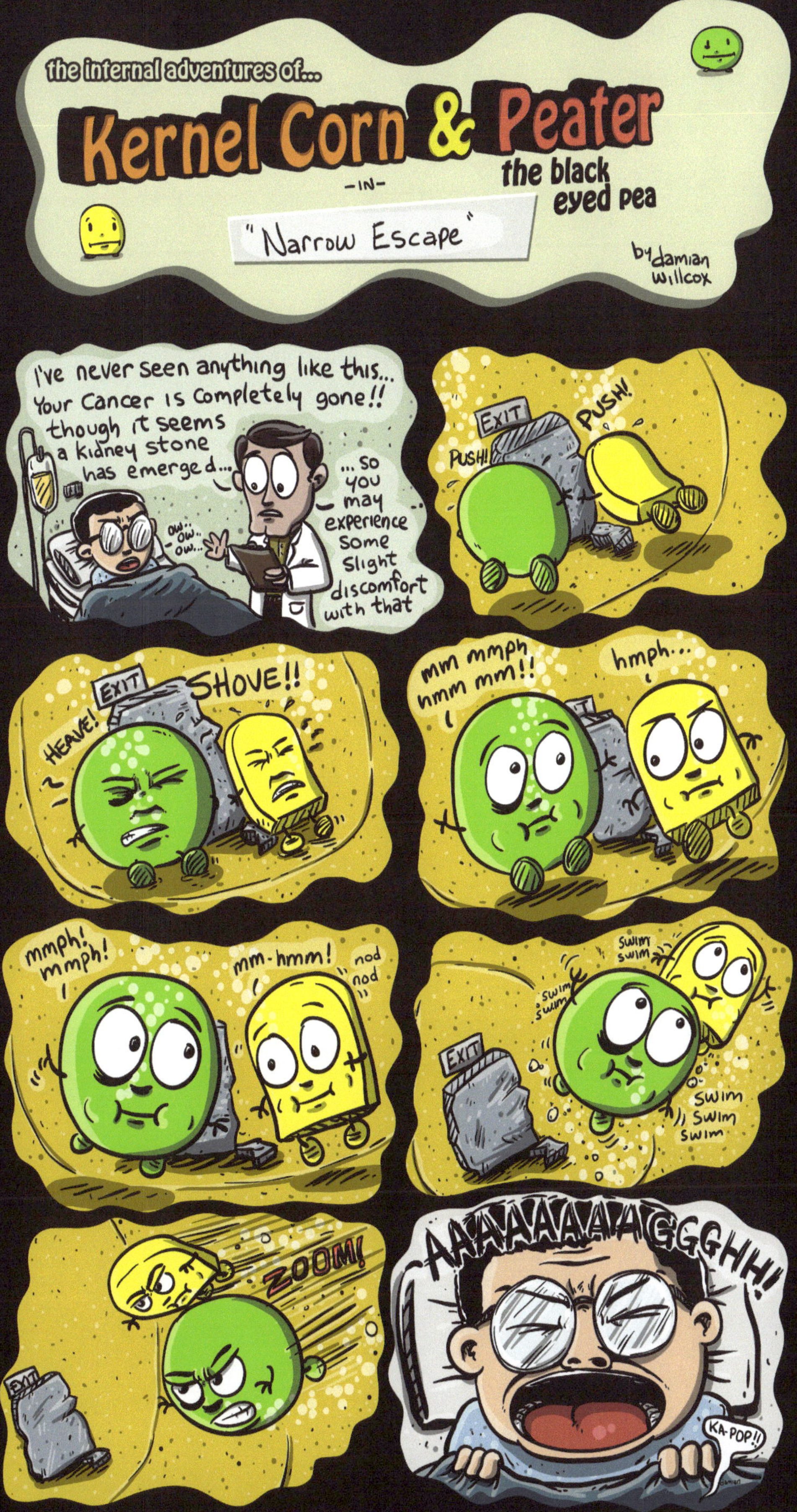

the internal adventures of...
Kernel Corn & Peater
-IN-
the black eyed pea
"Narrow Escape"
by damian willcox
I've never seen anything like this... Your Cancer is completely gone!! though it seems a kidney stone has emerged...
...so you may experience some slight discomfort with that
-ow.. -ow.. -ow...
EXIT
PUSH!
PUSH!
EXIT
HEAVE!
SHOVE!!
mm mmph hmm mm!!
hmph...
mmph! mmph!
mm-hmm!
nod nod
swim swim
swim swim
swim swim swim
EXIT
ZOOM!
EXIT
AAAAAAAAGGGHH!
KA-POP!!

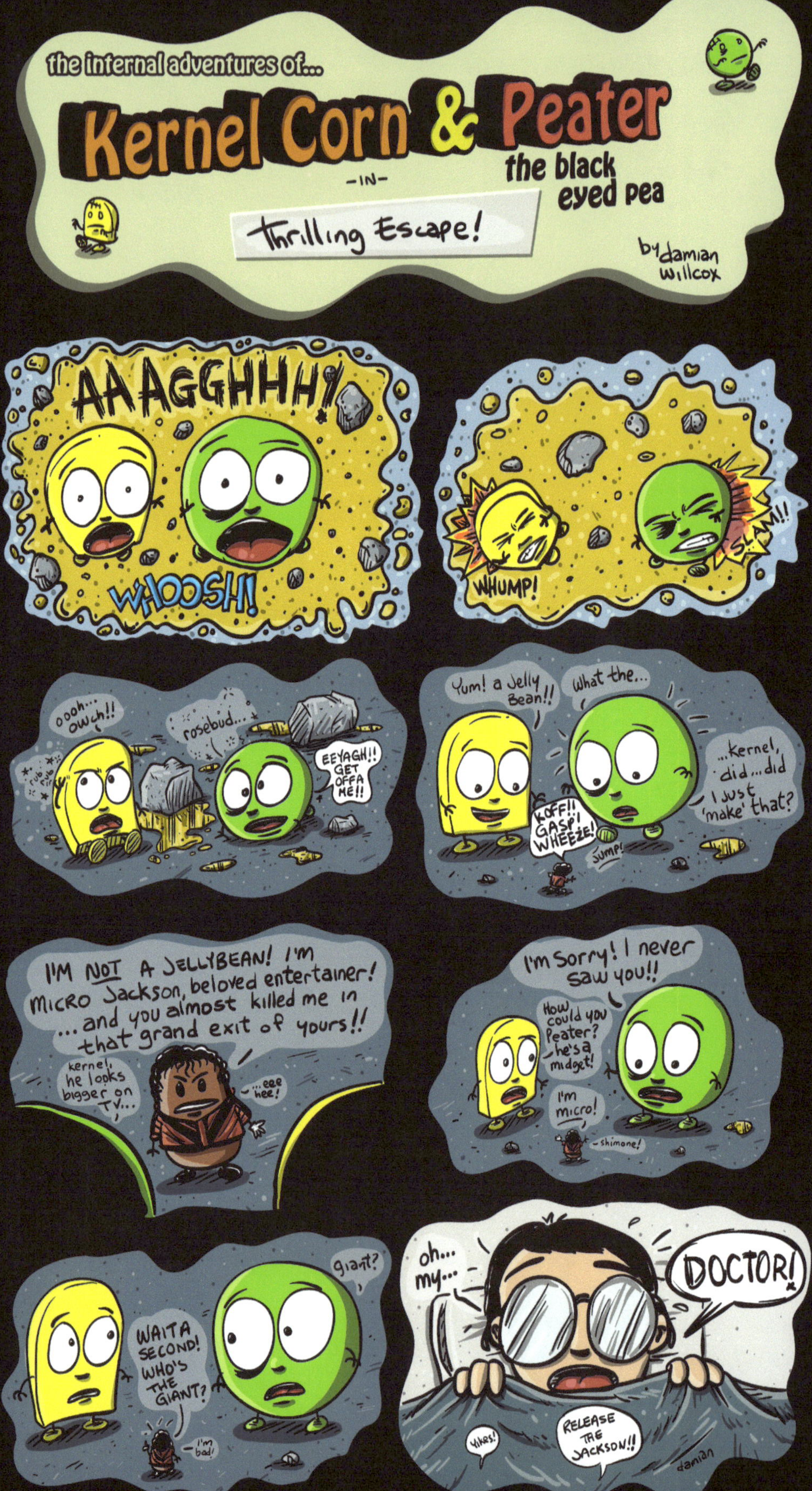
the internal adventures of...
Kernel Corn & Peater the black eyed pea
-IN-
Thrilling Escape!
by damian willcox
AAAGGHHH!
WHOOSH!
WHUMP!
SLAM!!
oooh... owch!!
rosebud...
EEYAGH!! GET OFFA ME!!
Yum! a Jelly Bean!!
What the...
...kernel, did...did I just 'make' that?
KOFF!! GASP! WHEEZE!
JUMP!
I'M NOT A JELLYBEAN! I'M MICRO JACKSON, beloved entertainer! ...and you almost killed me in that grand exit of yours!!
kernel! he looks bigger on TV...
...eee hee!
I'm Sorry! I never saw you!!
How could you Peater? he's a midget!
I'm micro!
-shimone!
giant?
WAIT A SECOND! WHO'S THE GIANT?
I'm bad!
oh... my...
DOCTOR!
YIKES!
RELEASE THE JACKSON!!
damian

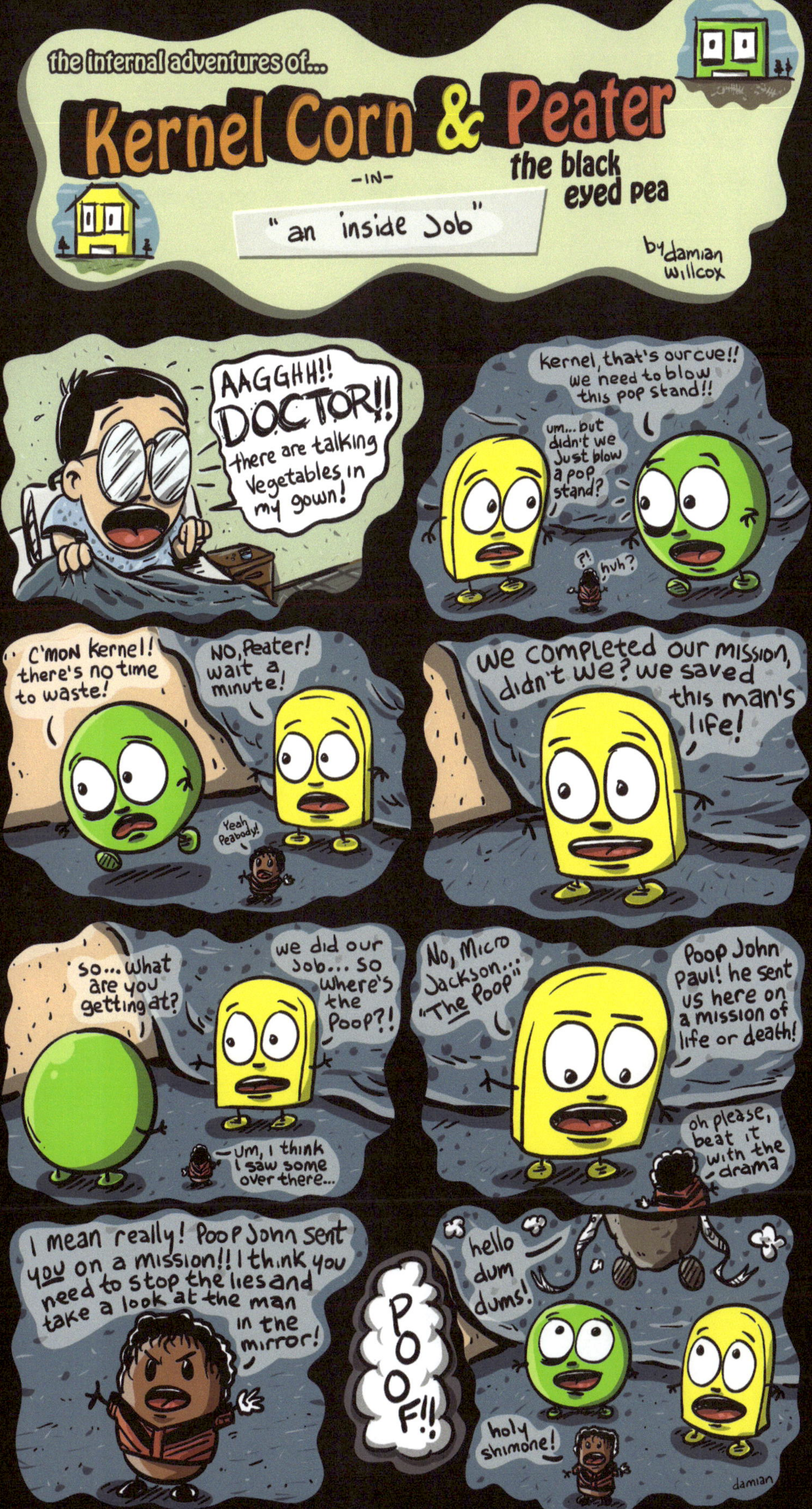

the internal adventures of...
Kernel Corn & Peater the black eyed pea
-IN-
"an inside Job"
by damian willcox
AAGGHH!! DOCTOR!! there are talking vegetables in my gown!
kernel, that's our cue!! we need to blow this pop stand!!
um... but didn't we just blow a pop stand?
?!
huh?
C'MON Kernel! there's no time to waste!
NO, Peater! wait a minute!
Yeah Peabody!
we completed our mission, didn't we? we saved this man's life!
so... what are you getting at?
we did our job... so where's the Poop?!
um, I think I saw some over there...
No, Micro Jackson... "The Poop"
Poop John Paul! he sent us here on a mission of life or death!
oh please, beat it with the drama
I mean really! Poop John sent you on a mission!! I think you need to stop the lies and take a look at the man in the mirror!
POOF!!
hello dum dums!
holy shimone!
damian

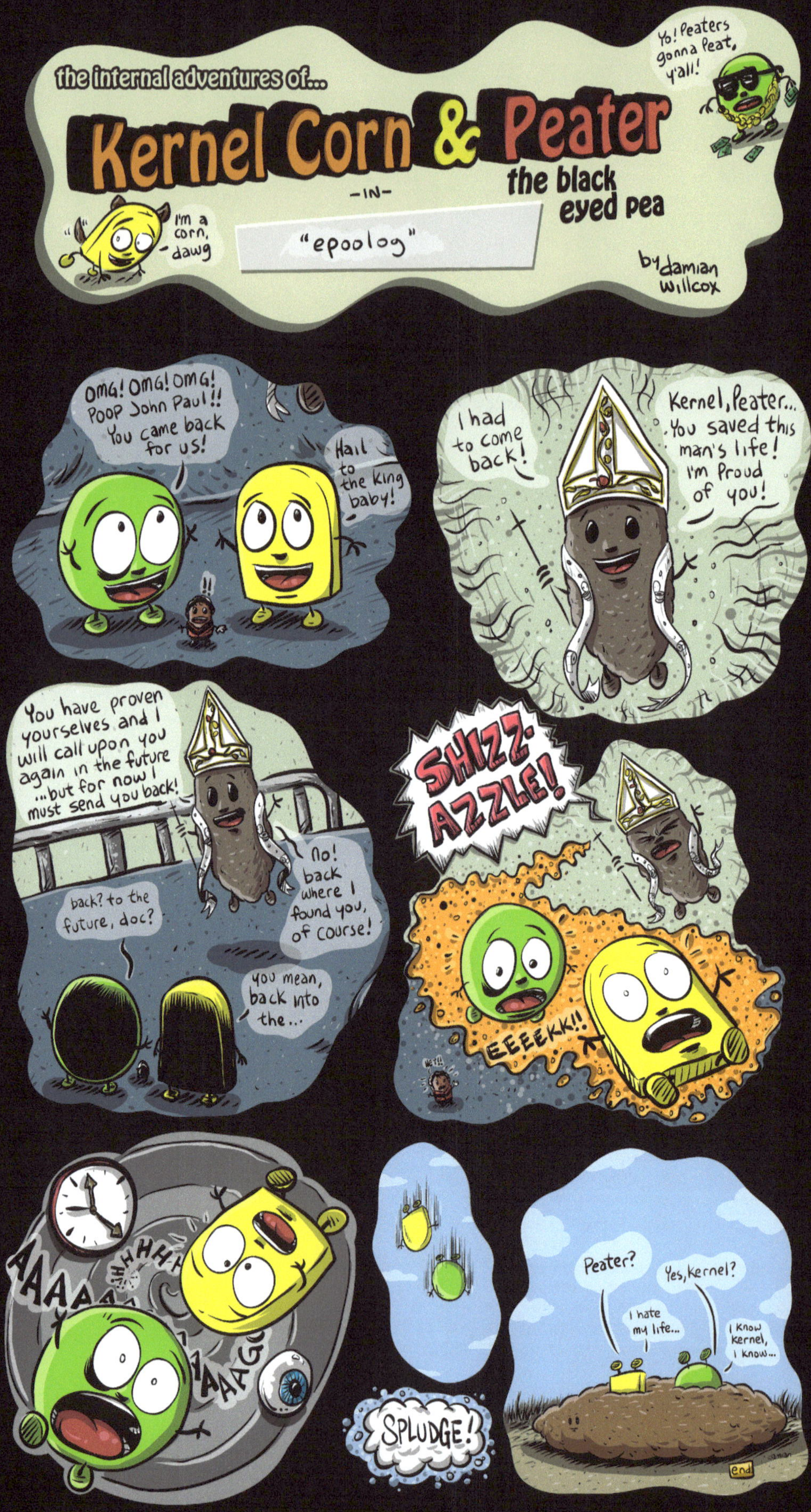
the internal adventures of...
Kernel Corn & Peater
-IN-
the black eyed pea
Yo! Peaters gonna Peat, y'all!
I'm a corn, dawg
"epoolog"
by damian willcox
OMG! OMG! OMG! Poop John Paul!! You came back for us!
Hail to the king baby!
I had to come back!
Kernel, Peater... You saved this man's life! I'm Proud of you!
You have proven yourselves and I will call upon you again in the future ...but for now I must send you back!
back? to the future, doc?
No! back where I found you, of course!
You mean, back into the...
SHIZZ-AZZLE!
EEEEKK!!
AAAAAHHHH
AAAG
SPLUDGE!
Peater?
Yes, Kernel?
I hate my life...
I know Kernel, I know...
end

sketches, paintings and the early years...

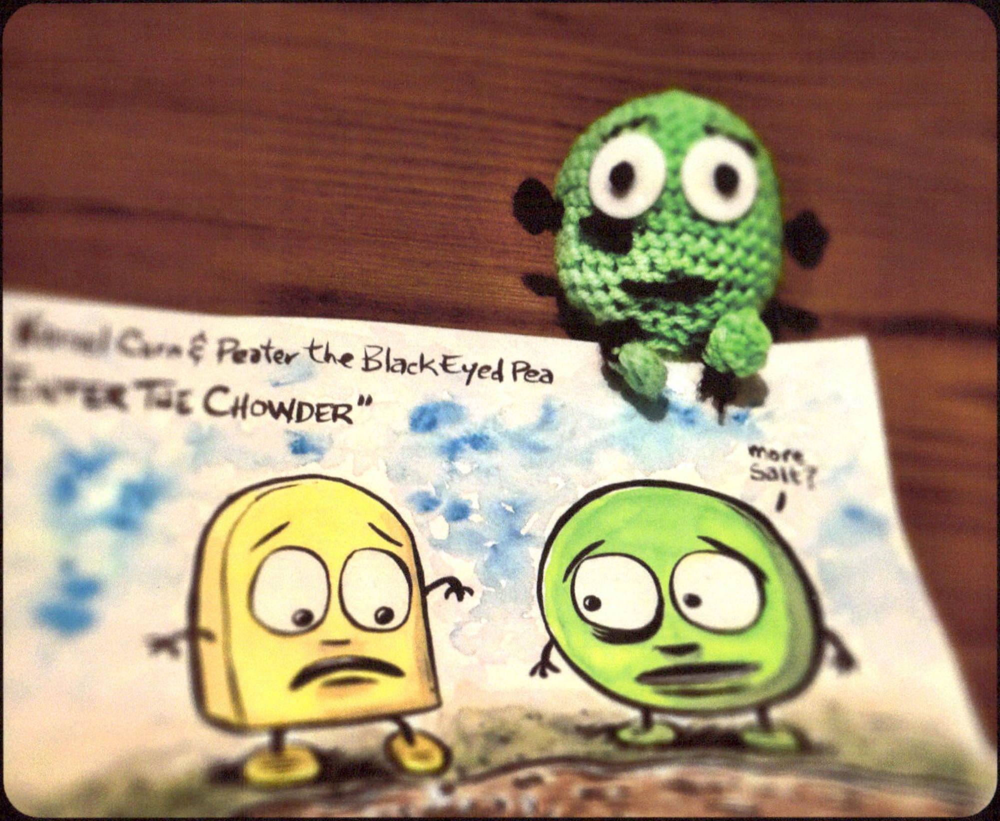
Corn & Peater the Black Eyed Pea
CHOWDER"
more salt?

My wonderful wife knit me this little Peater the Black Eyed Pea.

Here he sits on top of a watercolour and ink painting of Kernel Corn and Peater.

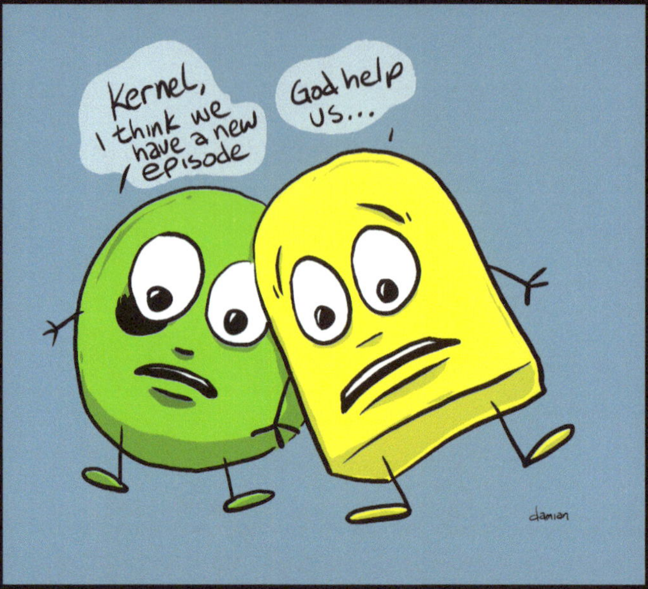
Kernel, I think we have a new episode
God help us...
damian

Sketch to announce the posting of new episodes on the site.

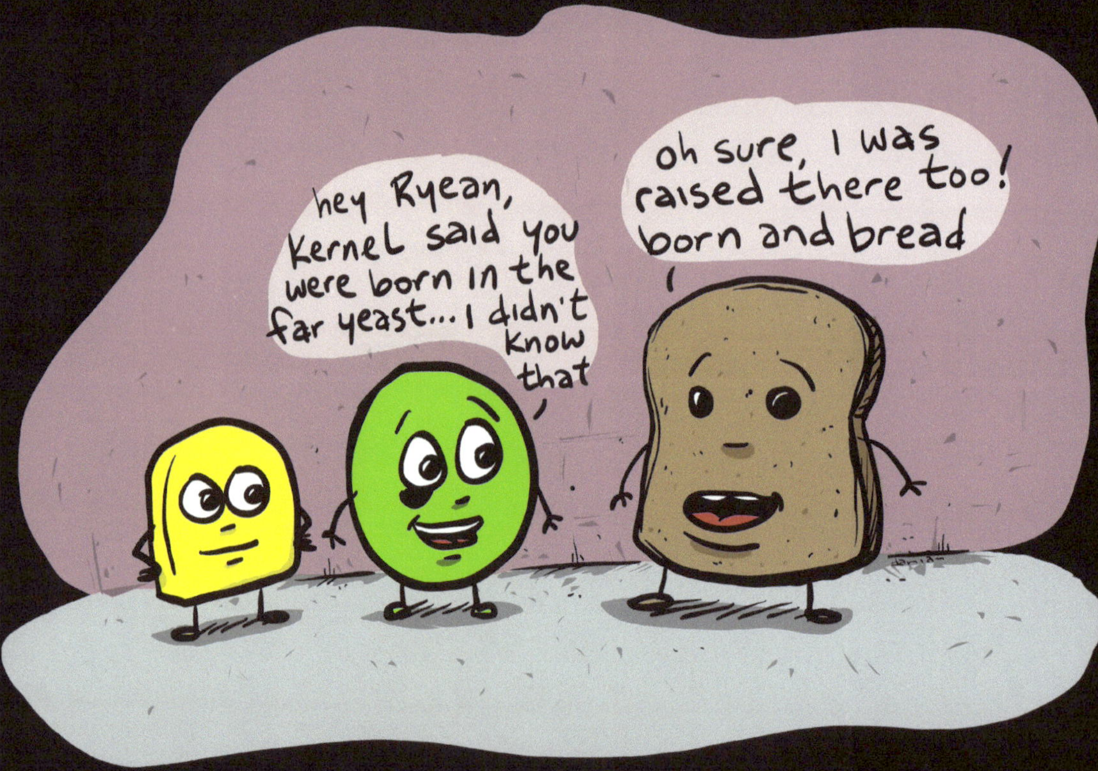
hey Ryean, Kernel said you were born in the far yeast...I didn't know that
oh sure, I was raised there too! born and bread

A one-off sketch/comic from the early years.

As a side note, pretty much every Kernel Corn comic in this book (this one included) was made completely start to finish in Adobe Illustrator - pencils, inks and colours.

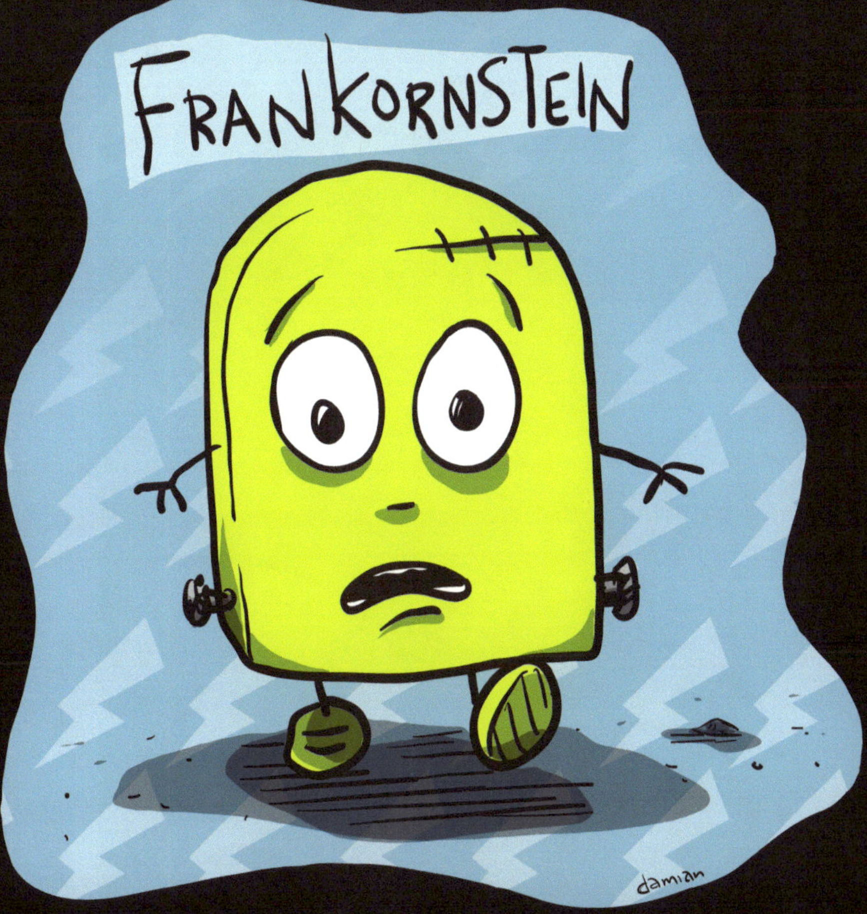
FRANKORNSTEIN
damian

Something tells me it may have been near Halloween when this was drawn.

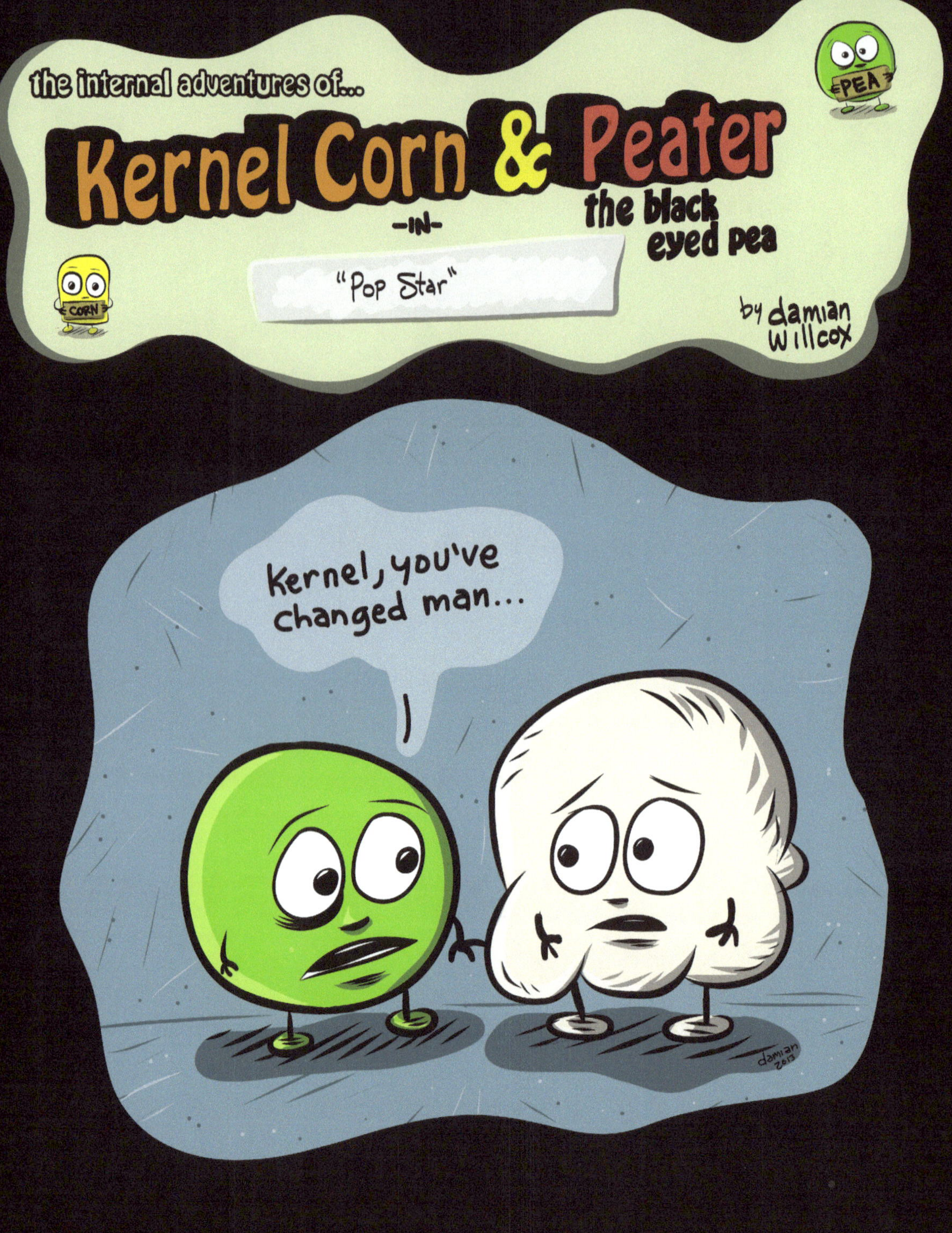
the internal adventures of...
Kernel Corn & Peater the black eyed pea
-IN-
"Pop Star"
by damian Willcox
PEA
CORN
Kernel, you've changed man...

A recent Kernel Corn comic drawn completely in the Adobe Ideas app started on my iPhone, and finished on my iPad while traveling to Japan.

Finally! Technology comes through for comic creation anywhere! Though I did have to redraw (trace) the header logo which was a pain.

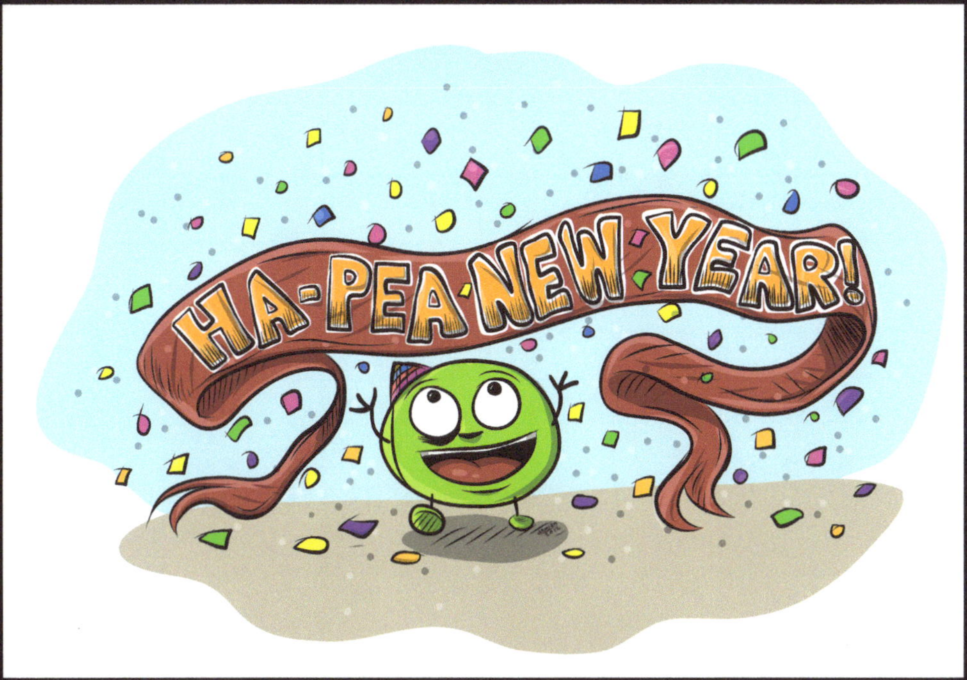
HA-PEA NEW YEAR!

A 2013 New Year's sketch drawn in the Adobe Ideas app on request by Adobe to be showcased on their Adobe Ideas app Facebook page.

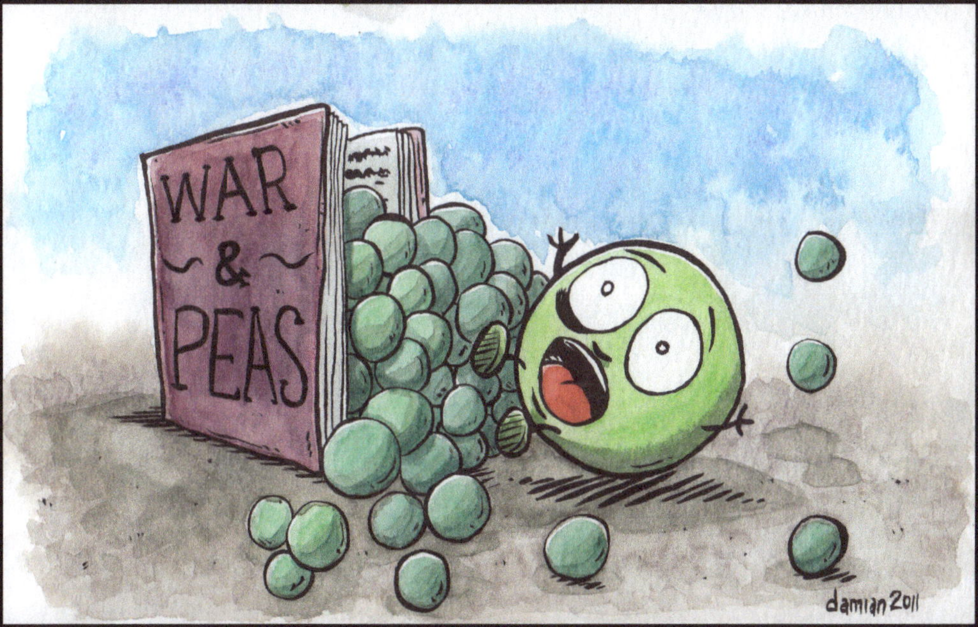
WAR
&
PEAS
damian 2011

"War & Peas"
(watercolour and ink)

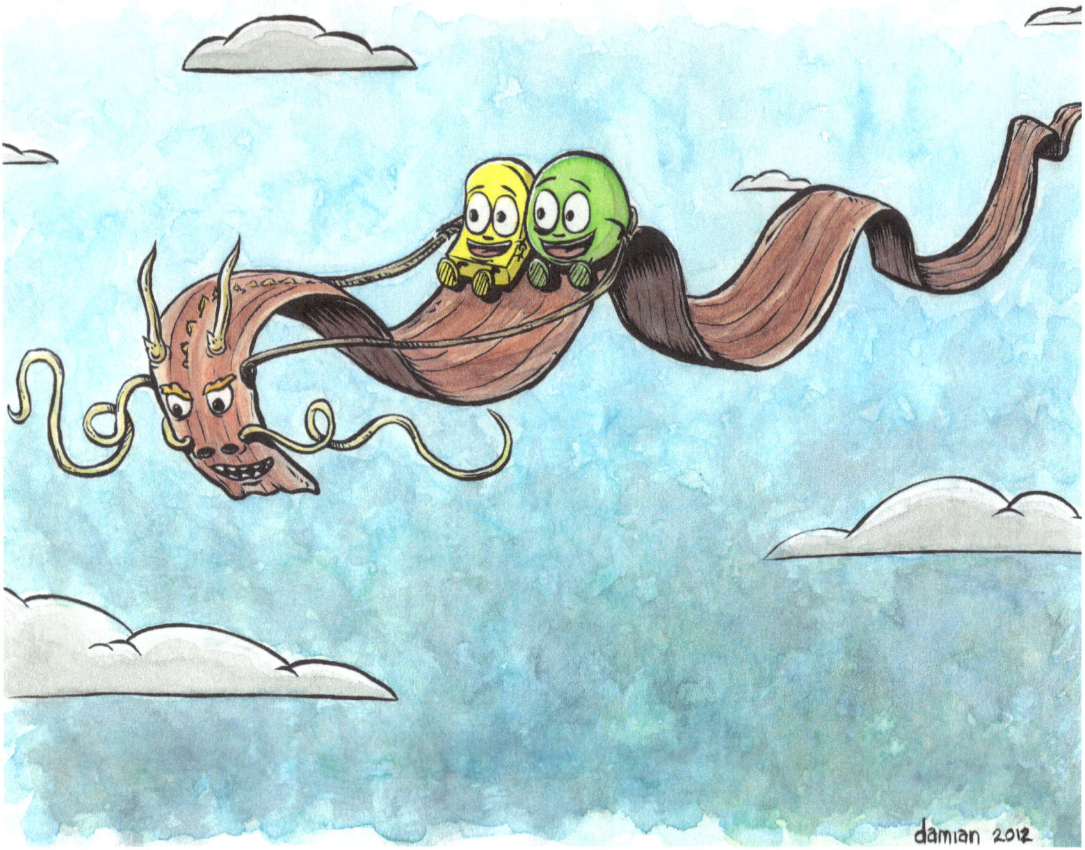
damian 2012

"Kernel Corn and Peater the black eyed pea meet the Bacon Dragon"

2012 was the Year of the Dragon.

For Kernel Corn and Peater, it was the year of the Bacon Dragon.
(watercolour and ink)

end note.

I've been making comics for quite a few years now, and am to this day still shocked and surprised by the support I get from fans like you.

I want to say thank you so much for picking up this book, and for being a hugely motivating factor in my work, I really appreciate it and it means a lot.

thanks,

♡damian

www.dorkboycomics.com
damian@dorkboycomics.com

"I love you, man!" 2012-12-29, 3:33 pm. Sanmesse, Nichinan, Japan

find me...

twitter:	@dorkboycomics
google+:	plus.dorkboycomics.com
facebook:	facebook.com/damiandraws
tumblr:	dorkboycomics.tumblr.com

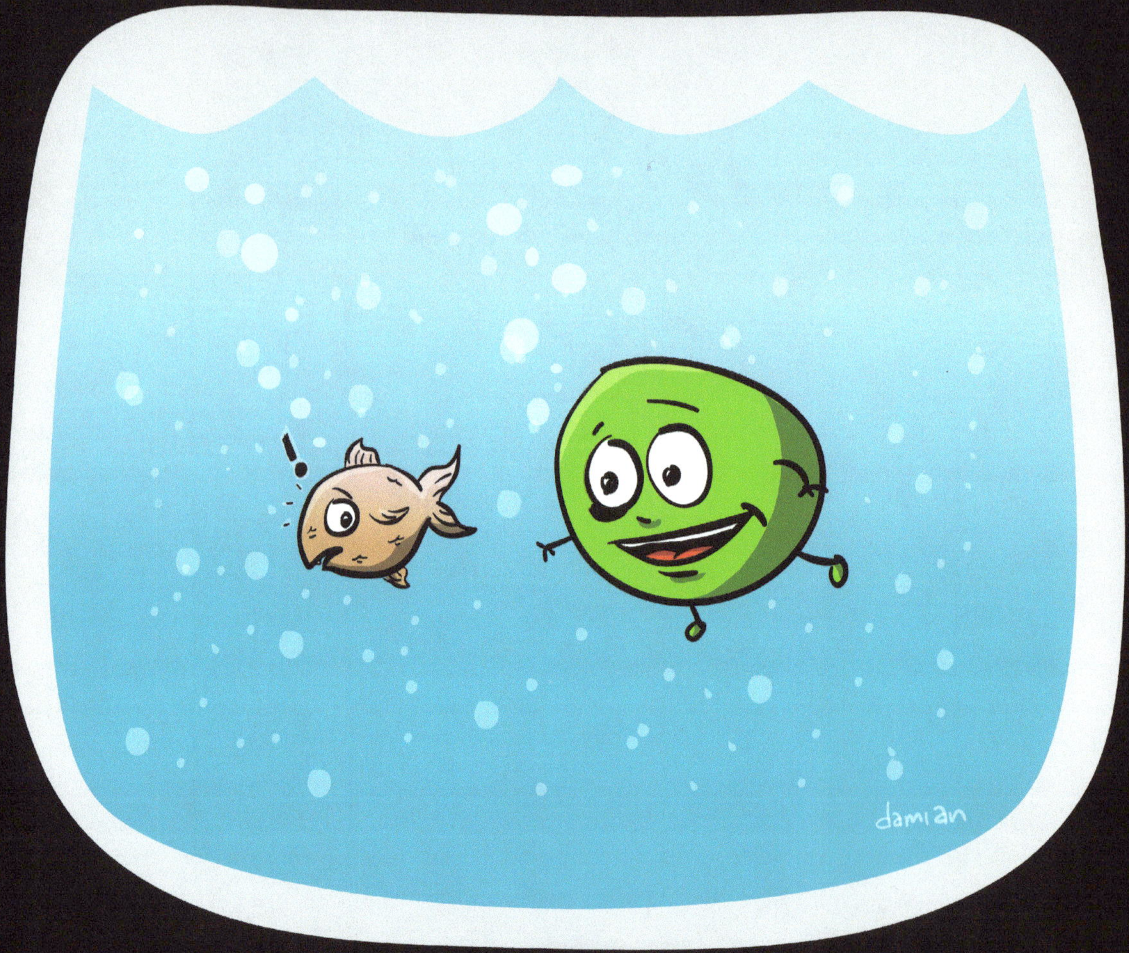
damian

One of my favourite Peater the Black Eyed Pea drawings.

Here's the best I can do in terms of an explanation:
I recall using corn as bait as a child when attempting fishing with my dad (we never caught anything), so I guess the logic follows that if corn attracts, then peas repel - no?

www.ingramcontent.com/pod-product-compliance
Lightning Source LLC
Chambersburg PA
CBHW040743110426
42739CB00028B/44